Fetch

TAMAR YOSELOFF was born in the US in 1965. Her first collection, *Sweetheart* (Slow Dancer Press, 1998) was a Poetry Book Society Special Commendation and the winner of the Aldeburgh Festival Prize. She received a New Writers' Award from London Arts for her second collection, *Barnard's Star* (Enitharmon Press, 2004). In 2005 she was Writer in Residence at Magdalene College, Cambridge, as part of their Year in Literature Festival. She is the Programme Co-ordinator and a tutor for The Poetry School. She divides her time between London and Suffolk, and is currently working on her first novel.

Also by Tamar Yoseloff

Barnard's Star (Enitharmon Press, 2004)
Sweetheart (Slow Dancer Press, 1998)

Fetch

Tamar Yoseloff

SALT

PUBLISHED BY SALT PUBLISHING
PO Box 937, Great Wilbraham, Cambridge PDO CB1 5JX United Kingdom

Salt Publishing 2007

Printed and bound in the United States of America by Lightning Source

Typeset in Swift 9.5 / 13

ISBN 978 1 84471 291 5 paperback

Salt Publishing Ltd gratefully acknowledges
the financial assistance of Arts Council England

1 3 5 7 9 8 6 4 2

Contents

Acknowledgements

Some of these poems originally appeared in the following publications: *Ambit, Chroma, Cimarron Review, The Liberal, Limelight, Magma, New Welsh Review, nthposition, Plant Care: A Festschrift for Mimi Khalvati, Poetry London, Poetry Review, Seam.*

My thanks to Tim Dooley and Sean O'Brien, careful readers and good critics. I am also grateful to the Fellows of Magdalene College, Cambridge, where I was Writer in Residence in 2005 and to Michael Harrison and the staff at Kettle's Yard.

I would also like to thank the following artists: Tim Lewis, for allowing me to quote his writings in 'The Angle of Error'; Julian Stair, whose funerary pieces inspired 'The Firing'; and especially Linda Karshan, for her friendship and collaboration, which culminated in the poem 'Marks'. Her series of woodblock prints, *One Day*, appears throughout this book.

Marks is also published as a limited edition Poetry Pamphlet and as an artist's book with images by Linda Karshan by Pratt Contemporary Art in 2007. www.prattcontemporaryart.co.uk

And my gratitude to Sheenagh Pugh, for sending me her Fetch.

Fetch

n. 1. A stratagem by which a thing is indirectly brought to pass, or by which one thing seems intended and another is done; a trick; an artifice.
2. C17: of unknown origin. The apparition or double of a living person; a wraith.

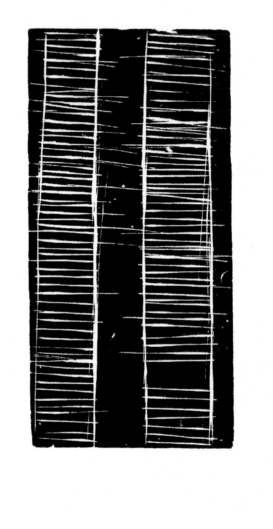

Fetch

I send her out
into the cold dark night.
She rides a bus to the edge
of town, enters a bar.

See her hair, nearly black
in the dim room, skin
translucent. She orders a beer,
downs it in one.

The men sit with their backs
against the wall, watch her
order another, cross
the floor, take a seat,

while I am safe
at home, wondering if I should
cut my hair — too long, I think
as I catch myself in the mirror.

She smiles at her reflection
in the jukebox, the glare of neon
like a halo, plays with a strand of hair,
chooses *Are You Lonesome Tonight?*

A quarter clinks into the slot,
the mechanical hand lifts
the black disc, slips it in place.
The arm swivels over

needle poised. The men
check out her ass, her legs.
Skirt's too short, I think,
pulling mine over my knees.

Polaroid

Far too bright, the Technicolor
version of my life, I shake it and
appear as if by magic, that happy child.

If I say *blue*, what do I mean?
An indigo sea, a lapis sky,
a mood too deep to fathom.

If I say *keepsake*, will you produce
a shock of hair held in a locket,
a blossom flattened in a book?

The brilliant moment drained to grey.
Faces rise from murky water,
undefined, the names have seeped away.

Black Water

I emerge from sleep, my tongue puddled.
You stand against the door, the light
behind you. You could be clay or iron,
I know your shape —

                              you were in my dream,
how clear you were—I could feel your touch.
We were in a house I haven't seen in years,
a shell—roof blown off, blackened eaves.

Long before you, places existed, objects
that have lost their definition.

I begin to focus. You are at the window.
I follow your gaze and see the clouds
clot on the horizon, a boat trailing its ghost,
the water's flat black surface, like ink or blood

and I think of the cold plunge,
                    water filling my mouth.

I run a bath, watch it curl with steam, then
ease myself in. Red spreads across my skin.

Illumination

Gold leaf, cadmium, ochre, saffron —
indelible once set on vellum.

The monks ground azurite and lapis
for perfect blue, took care

to cleanse their hands of poison
that made words sacred.

We place our fingers against
each other's lips, a vow of silence,

sense the touch mark even after.
I am brimming with words

but none can hold that moment
when our faces, edged in gold

glinted in the water's mirror,
the invisible sun within us —

so I let them fly, lead white
against a white sky.

Shadow

. . . how can a man throw his shadow, make this the illumination of his experience, how put his weight exactly—there?
— CHARLES OLSON

When we look back it is there, that
darkness of ourselves born
of days when the sun was blinding.

I trace what's left on the pavement
where you walked, schist or shit,
your heavy feet relearning those lost steps,

a dance we moved to once,
a shadow play in liquid streetlight,
late lamps, sodium glow of stars.

What mattered was matter, the precise
weight of you, so many ounces
of flesh and blood,

your hand on my shoulder, solid
and light like music,
our empty glasses on the table,

beakers for what cannot be
contained; the feather
of our lips, our touch.

The Seal

The horizon was low that day, the dull coast,
the curve of a mouth at the bay, the estuary flowing
to meet the sea. A weak sun, but it was late

when we arrived to an almost deserted beach;
wet sand sucked at our boots, then gave up their prints
in an instant—the way a beach

renews itself, a slate dragged clean by the pull
of the tide, the cycle of life and death and life
played small under rocks and in pools

swirling with opaque crabs, sea skaters,
a perfect ecosystem we disturbed to find our own rock,
smooth and flat, shaped to hold our bodies.

At first we thought he was another rock, just visible
on the surface, until he flipped over, one huge eye
a vitrine for the world beneath the waterline,

a shipwrecked treasure. He was the colour
of the stones you skimmed, your arm flashing out,
the colour of the rock we clung to, foam lapping our feet.

We sat there until shadows stretched the length of the shore
to the town, where people hurried along, held
in the tide of clocks and plans. The picture dissolves

like an underwater shell: the sky darkens, stars
rubbed out by cloud, the seal slips into an ink-black sea,
the memory of him sinking even as we take our leave.

Gorse

I breathe its scent, like sweat
on skin. The rain has brought it out.
Yellow settles on my scarf, too yellow,
a warning. Its branches shimmer water,
buds tight to bursting. Beyond the green stem,
its lobed leaves, I can see the thorns, daggered
in branches that anchor it to earth.
It owns this place.

I would like to plant
my fingers deep like roots, spread
like a dark stain, vigorous and hearty.
I would like to shed my petals, my silk touch,
before the final sharp prick
that draws blood. I trespass here,
I am only passing through. I close
my eyes and see an afterlight, a shock of yellow.

Spring

(after Barbara Hepworth)

Look at the way we
complicate our lives, shape
smooth hard surfaces, frame something
that gives, could collapse
if we're not careful.

                 We pull strings
taut, construct ourselves, little puzzles,
we have no end. But then the breeze rustles
the copper beech, everything's in bloom—
it could break our hearts.
                        Careful.

                 This stone is my anchor—
shimmering with tiny minerals,
beautiful in this light.
                   I must feel its heft
inside my palm, put my cheek
against its cool curve,
hold it close.

St Ives

And here we are again, the end of summer:
sky's a clean slate, a lighthouse leans
on its rock, coal smoke drifts over the toppled roofline.
The hills disappear, white on white, dull pearl
prised from an oyster.
                              The hierarchy of boats:
dinghies, trawlers, cruisers. Bobbing like apples
in a bucket. They imagine the open sea,
a voyage; they are tied to their moorings
with elaborate knots.

                              From this window: curtains
partly drawn, the coffee in the mugs
stone cold, the tiny union jack
the only colours in the world.

The Beginning of Winter
(after Laforgue, Bell and O'Brien)

I will go numb until summer, how else
to get through the next five months of rain?
The weatherman has a special map of Britain
just for this—black clouds over every city
and three over London.

Outside, buses slur their reds over tarmac,
slick coats pass with no heads, their owners
bent double in the wind, hoping to be blown
home, where the smell of cabbage is a comfort,
where the news is full of war again,

children go missing, pensioners go blue,
corporations sink; plus the usual Christmas reruns:
Morecombe and Wise, Tommy Cooper, Bob Monkhouse,
still living inside the TV, the ghosts of the front room.
No shaking the dead—they're on every channel.

I sleep all day, like the cat, and dream of rain,
a world turned flood plain, the joke
of a god who invented global warming, only here
it isn't warm. The leafless trees glisten,
their trucks silky with blackness.

And why go out? The shops are full
of jeans that are pre-distressed, with pre-made holes
(and I think of the girl on TV
shot trying to leave the settlement, lying in the road),
and, of course, camouflage again.

It will never stop—the rain, the war,
the test match (in rerun), the refugee
sent back, the rebranding, the market research,
the Brazilian supermodel, the kickback,
the freedom fries, the disgraced MP.

The rain is almost pretty, hanging
in lacy drops from the handrail, and I think
of it raining over the hills and into valleys,
on the tin roofs of makeshift factories,
on the postman as he delivers the mail,

on the funeral procession, the big parade,
the wino in the doorway, the M25,
the 747, a man I used to love, and it's comforting,
the democracy of everything being drenched
at the same time. God, give me the strength

for Spring, all that chirping and newness,
baby bunnies, too much pink. Let winter last
forever, now that I have settled into
the dark afternoon and central heating and the sharp note
of the singer as he moves into a minor key.

Interior with a Woman Playing the Virginals
Emanuel de Witte (c. 1660)

I played all morning, my fingers
light on the keys like birds. I wanted him
to love the full song I offered:

my husband was in the low countries
on business, this would never happen again,
I told myself, to have him so.

The maid kept busy in the hall, he stayed
behind the curtain while I played, but
I could smell him— frankincense, candlewax, sweat

and I swear it made my song dearer.
I played for him to keep him sweet,
I gave myself, like a sweetmeat on a plate.

He said words no man has said before,
and I was in love with him that moment
and for the hour he spent inside my chamber.

But a man like that is hard to hold, a bird
in the hand, so I let him go. He tipped his hat,
strolled into the afternoon. Now I am alone—

My chamber is as I'd left it,
the pitcher on the table full of daylight,
the mirror empty of a face,

and through the door,
the mop and pail wait patiently
to absolve the remnants of my folly.

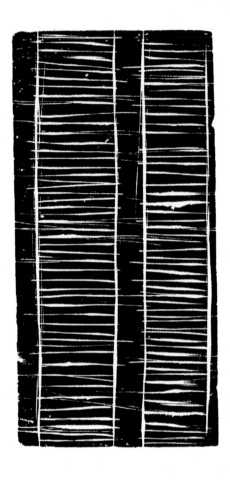

Fetch

I choose her uniform—
sunglasses, trenchcoat.
She needs to lose herself
in a crowd, to be invisible.

She enters Main Street
at 2:32 p.m. precisely,
sidewalk slick with rain,
sights him moving south.

Easy to spot in a crowd:
I'd know the arc of his shoulders,
his particular, easy gait,
from a mile away.

She must report
where he goes, who he meets,
if he still wears that blue shirt.
She's made for this,

tails him like a cipher,
a girl he might think
he knows from somewhere,
but can't quite place.

She keeps her distance
like I taught her, hugs the walls,
will duck into a doorway
the exact moment he turns.

He doesn't turn. He is a man
who never looks behind him,
although today, something
stops him in his tracks,

maybe a small prickle
of déja vu, like a finger
tracing the curve of his spine,
like someone treading on his grave.

The Firing

If I had any chance of recovery, this passion would kill me . . .
I have coals of fire in my breast.
                                        — JOHN KEATS

Our bodies, ignited by touch; however light,
flesh can singe with pleasure, the heart
can burn itself to cinder.

We leave relics in the sheets,
our sweat and skin, what's dead of us.
In the half dark I listen

for the shuttle of my heart.
Blood wells up through a cut
to taste the world.

I am a vessel, open
to your body. If only you could
move through me, enter

the spleen, the coiled intestine.
You are already in
my eye, my brain.

                ∿

Fire takes the manshape
like a lover: the clumsy arsonist,
the heroic father, the monk

in saffron robes. No matter
what they believed,
how they lived, in the end

reduced to this: a ribcage
forged in flame, curving
like the branches of a tree.

~

In the story my mother read me,
the tin soldier burned for love,
reduced to a molten heart,

the dancer's tinsel rose
shrivelled to a dark fist.
I longed for the happy ending.

Strange shapes would form
in darkness as I lay in my bed
at night, wondering

what it was like to die.
I found a bird's skull in the yard,
ran my finger over the beak,

the eyeless hole,
the smooth cranium,
then buried it in the ground.

~

A man stands before a wall
of fire, holding a cross
on a chain against his heart.

His likeness is on ivory
and although so small,
I think I see the flicker

in his eyes as he beholds
the woman who held
this image to her heart

four hundred years ago.
To think of the flame
he burned for her

snuffed out, four hundred
years in his grave, his love
reduced from flesh to bone

to soot; but flesh remains
in memory, the feel of her skin
beneath his fingers, like fine clay.

⁓

Coal and ironstone, silica, bole,
sea earth, marl, the soil yields
hard treasures, breaks down matter.

In the hill top cemetery the graves
fall in on themselves,
marble crumbles to dust,

loved ones tumble
into each others arms, their bones
knit and form a whole.

~

Gold fillings, titanium,
a wedding ring, calcium.
What doesn't burn

is sifted out. A light package
without heavy limbs
and troublesome heart.

When I die, scatter my ash
on water, so I curl the waves
on a cloud of dust,

each particle of me alive
to sunlight, floating,
a little boat of myself.

Vaporetto in Winter

The chill air, the sill of the Mediterranean—
I dream I'm Ottoman, in brocade and ermine,
sailing into the Bacino.

A woman holds her chihuahua aloft like a delicacy,
the men argue weather with their hands,
the Salute floats like a tethered balloon.

To the South the Giudecca curves like a grin,
its blinds pulled low to sun, gardens still
behind high walls, the smell of bread and refuse.

To the North, the Zattere unfolds
its long parade of workers, children, tourists;
the gelateria is closed for business.

At Santa Marta, liners coax themselves into port,
shivering in twilight. We tip into the Chiara,
trains going nowhere on the sidings.

The distant flame of Porta Marghera sets fire to the sky.
Frankincense of Arabia, opium of China, conquered
by the molten steel of America.

The Library

The fire was never lit. Cold, her body
was alert to words, her pores open to knowledge.
Sealed off from the rest of the house, padded
with paper and board, the only sound was the turning
of the page, a whisper, her shallow breath.

Gone. The books scattered to far corners,
cities a thousand miles away, strange
against paperbacks with rainbow covers,
they still carry the scent of deerskin and beeswax,
mildew—travellers from an antique land.

The model ship that used to drift the dark oak desk
is lost, never to reach the new world,
never to return home. She would touch
its windless sails, wonder at how they could make
everything so small. A planet reduced.

The Visitants
for Mimi Khalvati

> *. . . I attract them the way*
> *I do children: a whole orphanage of elephants*
> *on presents, cards, surrounds me on my birthday*

I can see them now—crossing savannahs,
tree-legs flattening the pampas grass,

the parched deserts, forests of the tropics,
to come to you in London. They converge

in Piccadilly Circus, dwarfing Eros,
each footfall sinking craters in the tarmac

so when it rains the roads will brim with lakes.
They amble down Fleet Street, buses faltering

in their wake. They navigate the alleys
of Spitalfields, its ancient houses shaking,

they enter Hackney in a fluster of tusks
and traffic, mini cabs blaring their angry horns,

but they are not daunted. They find you at home,
cradle you in their silken trunks, sweep you

into a howdah and bear you through the city
like a deity. They bat their eyes like girls,

dance the joy dance, spin, and flap their ears,
but you can hear the ocean of sadness they carry:

they never forget the land where they were born,
the bitter taste of heat and ash on their tongues,

the sweet fruit, overripe to bursting,
so strong in them that they open their mouths and sing.

They call to you in the velvet night and you wake,
humming a tune you know, but cannot place.

Tiger

He stalks the wilds of the duvet
in this nil-star hotel room,
just a double bed and a bidet.

On the street, the ladies of the Barbès
saunter in five-inch heels, buy
Medjool dates, long okra fingers,

the men bask in a cloud of Gauloises,
drink sweet coffee that leaves a sludge
in the cup. Two floors up

you sing to me of drunken sailors,
whores straddling the harbour;
your fingers tease guitar strings.

I whisper to you how the foie gras
slipped down my throat,
the Sauternes, silk on my tongue.

Beneath the tiger's eye, your hand
is moving up my thigh. I am all
polished spruce, catgut,

you make me sing. We recreate ourselves
as Cubists, intersect tongues and limbs,
pliant and supple, animal.

Shallott

There was a girl once
who could speak three languages,
who knew plant names and could type.
She had fair hair that fell into her eyes.
Maybe she died. The woman
who lives here now is bone-thin, worn
like this shattered plate. She rages
at the weeping tree, her weary breasts.
She knows about blood, considers
how to summon it, lovely potion—
the razor and its buttery touch,
the cough that brings it up, shining
on a white handkerchief. She craves its
sticky taste; runny honey, spunk.
She wanders the streets, feels
the riverbed swell under her feet.
She sees men watching her, eyes
like questions, remembers their hands
sliding over her as if she were glass.
She can undress them, feel their pricks
growing in her hand, vessels of blood.
At night she hears the blackbird—
lovesick, lightpoisoned—singing his
heart out, the fox crying to no one,
her fur bristling in the cold, and she flies
out of her body to meet them,
her barge balanced over the city
in a bolt of lightning.

Fungi

If we think dishonestly, or malignantly, our thoughts
will die like evil fungi—dripping corrupt dew

— JOHN RUSKIN, *Proserpina*

The smell—
wet anorak, fusty books, disturbed dust
of long unopened doors—
like the basement of your childhood,
beautiful scary darkness.

They poke
their tiny heads through dirt,
explorers from another age, and find
a world glassy with rain, a forest
thick with leaf mulch.

A good one,
if you're starving, could save
your life. A bad one would kill you
after only one bite. Step on its poison head,
it billows black fumes.

Lost in the woods
and hungry, how to tell them apart?
You can trust the feel of flesh on your tongue,
good meat—you know it won't hurt you,
you're a bit of a witch yourself.

Fetch

I am thinking of her
constantly, the way she walks—
someone once told me
I walk on my toes—

the way she holds a pen—
I have a ridge on my finger
where my biro rubs—
the way she writes him down:

He's drinking coffee, his thin lips
grazing the side of the cup,
the contents still hot, his mouth
making little kissing motions.

He smells of cut grass
and tobacco, runs his fingers
through his hair, gazes into
the distance, as if he's seen a ghost.

That was her last report.
Somehow she's managed
to throw me—she's learned
the principles of treachery—

now I wait for them both
to return, counting the hours
like a rosary, the pang
of loss pressed on my ribs.

Siesta

for Chris and Marisa North

The rain arrives, decides to stay. It spills
over the terraced hills, drenches the rooster
into silence, floods the roofless villa,
slicks the skins of the persimmon. It hazes
the distant peaks, rides the rapids of the pool,
drives us to our rooms. We chase the cat
from the chaise longue and curl up into sleep.
Daylight drains to evening, an ancient dark,
we wade through airless halls with shuttered windows,
the distant boom of thunder. It will end soon
the weathermen say; we know it will last forever—
we find ourselves submerged in a mire
of speechless hours, when even the clock
can't be bothered to chime.

The Blue Moon

A rare phenomenon, the astronomers said.
Amateurs raced to the hills with astrolabes
and planispheres, while in the city
weathermen predicted high visibility.

We took to the roof and waited; planes and stars
glittered in the haze, until a crescent moon
curved the sky, its shadowed whole blooming
indigo, as darkness drew in—a moon

anchored by ocean, as if it would float
through the cosmos, and we might skim
its hidden surface, might be submerged
by blueness. All night we sat there,

until the moon faded, replaced by a grey sun,
an unremarkable morning; but we were different—
an opal tinge had graced our skin.
We moved through the afternoon slowly,

not to break the spell. Experts spoke
of sunlight scattering from earth
onto the lunar plain, while a man in the street
preached the end of the world.

The Venetian Mirror

When I first hung it in our bedroom we could not sleep all night,
it was like having the moon for company, so bright it shone
— JIM EDE

1.

Silver has its day, recedes
to reveal the surface beneath

gone black—
its own Dorian moment.

It reflects back what we have
not been able to understand,

an abundance lost, just hinted
in the etched leaves, tendrils lacing

the frame. What's inside is
rust, a pox on a lovely face,

still we trade its dimensions
for our own: dumbstruck, vain.

2.

The basilica behind a slick
of rain, gold diminished

to dun. The colour of nothing.
The bulk of it jagged

on the darkening sky.
The end of day, odic light

illuminates a shrivelled rose;
all the sadness we contain

in this drop of rain, its
crystallised gloom.

3.

The ghost hulk of the palazzo
leans into the canal. Narcissus crazed.

Tarnished jewels, pink marble
dulled to flesh. Shiver of a ballroom

out of season, sliver of broken
glass, the first glistening of frost,

as the campana strikes,
mourns itself in echo.

The Angle of Error

This is a more complex geometry than I had intended

I have charted this on my graph of unease—

your hand in motion—
    push, twist, splay

the arrowed grass in a rain-soaked field, each blade defined—

    the grey stone of disappointment.

Your face picassos—
    I can no longer picture you whole.

An endless spirograph of a narrow room, an off-season coast—

    my head slanted to catch your mouth
your hand sphering my wrist—

    the gazetteer of hurt.

I think I'm moving forward
    but I'm not

my heart pounding its old song—*stop, stop, stop*

navigating a tiny circle
    a crutch dragged in the dirt.

Road

for Catherine Smith

The wheel is a lizard in your hands.
You have seen lizards flattened like in cartoons—
they don't spring back to life. And hubcaps,
glittering in the ditch, the eyes
of a tin-can monster.

The map unfolds:
        paper transformed to desert,
names grown into towns, but the last town
passed you by—a clutch of houses,
empty corner store, City Limits teetering
on the edge of nothing—several days back.

You had plans once,
opinions, but now you are silent.
The road speaks a language of tar and rock
you must concentrate to understand.
There's a zincy ting in your mouth.

The road will always be
driving you. It gives off a false sense
of warmth, it will not take you home.
It knows you are in love
with its hard surface, its flatness, its endless black line.

The Dentist

He runs his thumb slowly over the peaks
of lower molars, cupping my chin in his palm,
over that stubborn incisor that refused
to be straightened. He rubs the sharp canine

and I bite down, involuntarily, trapping the ball
of his finger in a cage of teeth. *Open* he says,
and I do, *wider*, until he can probe the delicate cave
of my throat, pink and ridged, the glistening uvula,

a bell clap silenced, the soft carpet of tongue
and palate. He pulls my lips apart, his face
so close, I can see a line of stubble along his chin,
the fine pores, his perfect startling teeth.

He is trying not to breathe, and I am trying
not to swallow, as my saliva rises around his
finger, a foreign body. He inserts his mirror
to examine my every crevice, my tongue catches

the taste of metal, like blood, the cold touch
of the instrument, and he wants me to open even
wider, until I feel my jaw unhook like a snake
ready to swallow its prey. It seems to last forever;

my jaw begins to ache with the labour
of opening, and staying open, my juices dried
like a river bed consumed in the heat
of the interrogating sun. *You can close now,*

he says, as he moves the beam from my face.
I blink and find he's planted himself behind
my eyes, so when I shut them, he remains.
Your teeth are beautiful, he says. *Now rinse.*

Lamb Pasanda

The soft breath of evening rain on glass
mists the picture window. A sitar sings;
she sits beneath a canopy of stars.

He brings her spicy popadoms, a glass
of cabernet; the lime pickle stings
her tongue. Lamb Pasanda garnished with stars

of cardamom. Above her, behind glass
the image of Kama, his sugar arrows stringed
with flowers, his beloved Rati starry

in his grasp. So starstruck, she could sing.

Silk

Glissando   the small
shimmer of my sashay.
Ssh, or you'll miss me.

       You'll miss me,
the cool dip as I slip
from your fingers:

the one that got away.
A miraculous fish,
all glide and guggle,

as I dive into my sea
of troubles.
              You've only
skimmed the surface.

I wear this, precious gift
of industrious worms,
       so I'm engrained

in your memory, like
the green light, red room,
the geisha gloom

of black silk   slick
under your fingers
as you undo those

fiddly little buttons
one by one, and open me:

a Pandora's box,
a bag of tricks,

a billet-doux
addressed to someone else.

Portrait of a Couple Looking at a Turner Landscape

They stand, not quite touching,
before a world after storm.

There are drops of moisture in her hair,
in his scarf
           the colour of a gentler sea, his eyes,

while trains depart every minute, steaming
into the future, where the hills

unroll themselves,
vast plains of emerald and gold

      (she undressed for him, slowly,
        her skin like cloud under dark layers)

after rooms of Rubens and Fragonard, flesh dead
against old brocade
          (their flesh alive in the white sheets).

There are trains departing.
          When they part
it will be night, outside a theatre, near the station,

     and the sky will be blown with stars,
too dim to see in the glare of neon.

They will stand on concrete and asphalt,
          the innocent shining sands

lost. The world tilts to meet her face,
he holds her face close

    and something closes in on them,
the weight of silence in the street,

the winter horizon, bright, huge,
the moment before
        the sky opens and it pours.

The Red Hill

(after Elisabeth Vellacott)

The midmorning ridge, dreaming
fields. Harvest. A harvest moon
last night, and today, a hare
balanced on the edge, briefly.

Remember this. It may not
come again, the razor sky,
the trees, rust and leaves
in the air. Perfect stillness.

Commit it to yourself
so that it enters your blood,
returns as a heartbeat
the second before you move

forward, and it is shattered.
Your mark will be erased
by wind, hard rain,
by the way you race

from one place to another,
wanting so to lie down,
to fit the earth around you,
taste the ferrous clay.

Remember this, before
it shifts to brick, asphalt,
to a white curtain, a bare room;
many rooms will clutter your head.

Beyond the ridge, the little house,
the fire lit. In it are people
you love. They are waiting.
You close your eyes

and the field breaks into lines,
a sketch of a field, it blurs
and aches, gives way
to white. You fill in the rest.

Fetch

After days, I spy her
in the lobby of a motel,
wearing my brown coat.
She smoothes it over her hips,

determined, steely. I want to
shake her by the shoulders,
the shape of her bones familiar,
but it's too late.

When he sees her, his face
changes completely as if he
has never seen her, as if he
has seen nothing else.

He says *your hair is different*,
and runs his fingers through it,
I can feel the crush of his lips
as he pulls her close by my collar.

In a room on the third floor
she unbuttons his shirt (the blue one),
spreads her hand full
over his chest, his coarse hair

blossoming under my fingers.
She has stopped breathing. He is hard
against her, pushes her legs apart
I have stopped breathing.

On the wall above the bed,
a faded Monet poster:
a girl in a white hat
adrift in a field of poppies.

As their bodies blur in the tangle
of bedclothes, I feel my skin
go numb; the power to receive
his touch is gone, his face goes dark.

She has found herself without me.
I am stranded in a station
at midnight, where the train
rushes through without stopping.

Voyage

The train sails through fields, docks in middle-
manager cities: Coventry, Milton Keynes,
the track before us a fact of our expansion,
the night inevitable—sick phosphorescence of lights
coming on, of platforms rushing past,
the names of towns illegible with speed,
their tower blocks blown back in a sudden squall.
On the page a man is drowning:
I only have to close the book to forget him.
He's history. The present is about the train
hurtling past on the opposite track, steering
for where I've just been; the flotsam of travel:
the paper cup, the empty miniature,
the folded tabloid. Old news. Salt on my tongue.

Marks

If you think of the forms and light of other days, it is without regret
— SAMUEL BECKETT

1.

I have marked
      the clock's   black arm
winter movements   of the stars

where you left off speaking
      traces of you   in all things—

the white space where you were
      standing

      all explodes around you
         an invisible halo—

angel of dust   and light

the spiders   understand
      weave intricate maths in the eaves
      hatch   in the artificial heat

while outside
      winter   my winter haunt

I have this in my body
coldness

the ice   breaks
a song   in the trees

fingers of condensation
     drag the windows clean

what I see   I have always seen

you were always
             in front of me
blocking the light

2.

Blades of grass through snow—
                        snow falling

flakes on my tongue
cold kiss

I used to do this
when I was a girl   my mouth
                           open to the sky

things don't join up now

I track the prints
of some animal   through the white

hieroglyphs
in a field
                        they trail off

             I have followed the wrong lead

my pulse
a little morse of blood

             any more than this
             I can't make out

3.

A finger blades a line
straight   from throat to womb

peel back my skin   reveal
          the workhouse   of heart and lung

          blood
slogging   through my veins
          my discontented bones

4.

all that inner space   *one never sees*
        the brain and heart
and other caverns   places where marks
        don't show

        not like skin
                it carries every cut

        those prints flower like a bruise

I turn   turn again
        show my good side   the good side
it's never the same twice

        myself in my skin
        what I understand

all that inner space
        and no way out
                the bars become a window
through which to see yourself

I will return to
        the scene of my betrayals
        the kindly dark

5.

Slice the dark
     my razor   margin of error

no maps—

watermarks
fingerprints
Roman road beneath the field   old earth
   a page
      erased

we unsleuth/ unsheaf
     cut a path with our bare hands

no guides—

reservoir covered over
memory of water
the night
     recovered

trial and error   we find the centre

6.

Hold it in your hand
hold it to the light

    bird   bone
      breaker
           stone
delicate crevice of ice—
          broken

      beaker
          hone
      high   held
        blight
throw it to the sea
hold it tight

delicate surface of bone—
       old white

7.

Radio waves in air
        break over me

words
    just audible
between broken frequencies

sound   without
    meaning

I mean

the sky darkens to hold
    its weather

to go on   and get on
    my only care

what holds us here
    is weather
        whether or not   we are

8.

A box of snow
      the moment

I melt away
      an echo   of myself

words are
      light

they hold no ice
      wise   crack

a long white turnpike
      a road   to no—

9.

My mark on the page
                    a smudge

my voice   breaks up
      down the wire

long   distance
                    we can't bridge this

the margin is
                where you set it

open the book   see
            words   as horizontals

cross   word
                    here's where you draw the line

words at sea   an   s   o   s

10.

I will return to
the broken bone
the open page
the house of ice
the radio waves
the wave goodbye
the morse of blood
the winter trees
the frequencies
the clock's black arm
the wounded path
the Roman road
the spider's web
the ocean bed
the weathervane
the chance of rain
the fractured line
the fretted light
the box of snow
the flowered bruise
the empty room
the blades of grass
the razor's gash
the old cold kiss
the body's slog
the touch of skin
the heart the heart
the kindly dark

The Butley Ferry (off season)

A rowboat marooned in the mud until Spring,
its prow thrusts towards the opposite shore,
shallows spotted with oystercatchers
teetering on red stilts, terns, and we turn

towards an indifferent sky—hard to tell
what season we are in—the colour of the mud
that wants to hold us in its grasp. Nothing to stop us
from ferrying ourselves across;

the trusting boatman has left the oars
folded like waiting arms inside his boat.
Beyond the riverbank the Ness
stretches a thumb across Orford Harbour,

silent now, its unexploded bombs
patient beneath the frozen ground,
the pagodas like foreign girls who breeze
through town in summer; and beyond, the sea.

But the water is so black, the wind is picking up;
not a day to make a journey, not even
to the other side. We turn back, retrace our steps
to the last field. The bullocks watch us,

swaying on their skinny legs, their long babyfaces
so serious, chewing on hard grass, chewing,
their eyes like chunks of obsidian,
precious and cold.

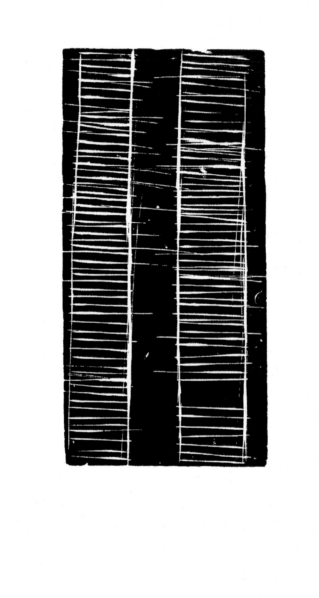

Fetch

It can only end
one way—on the edge of town
on the darkest night I can imagine,
and she's alone. So alone

she can feel the ache rising
from stomach to heart to brain.
She has lost us both. I knead the vein
on the side of my head, throbbing.

I knock a whisky back,
she feels a burning
in her throat. This is going to be
hard, I think, steering her

away from the safety
of a street lamp, into the unknown.
At the other end of the street,
a car swerves into being

takes the edge off the corner
onto the sidewalk.
She will never know
what hit her.

The Sea at Aberystwyth

This is the end
of the world. The wild west, but not the frontier.

The old monster is roaring on the beach again—
kids run along the front in shirtsleeves, chasing

his fury, one great dark wave after another.
Oh rain, wash them clean.

The Norwegian tourists bask in a thousand ways
of getting wet. The windows of the Marine Hotel

are caked with guano. Maybe the rain will do the trick.
The seagulls swerve in the air stream.

The Spice of Bengal dims its lights, its one customer
sated. Time to wander into night. What we want

lies broken on the shore, what we can't have
stays black on the horizon;

the moon of the zebra crossing
flashing for no one.

Printed in the United Kingdom
by Lightning Source UK Ltd.
R679400001B/R6794PG120135UKX1B/1-24

Whilst I believe that by working together through this method,
we are optimising your chances of having a baby, there is no guarantee.

The only thing I can guarantee is that if there is a block,
we will find it and we will unlock it.

Contents

DR LOUISE GODDARD-CRAWLEY is a chartered psychologist with over 20 years' experience working as a health professional. With a special interest in the psychology of health, Louise works from her private practise in Marylebone seeing a varied range of mental health presentations. Louise works with a number of women, men and couples who have been affected by infertility and miscarriage. Her focus on fertility stems from her experience with a leading London fertility clinic, where she worked as the deputy nurse manager for a decade. It is this unique marriage of her experience at the clinic coupled with her psychology training that has led to this book.

Louise completed her first degree in Health & Human Sciences in 1994, where she qualified as a nurse. She worked as a nurse in a variety of settings, spending a number of years working in A&E. Very much like the essence of the book, she then focused her attention from the physical towards the psychological and undertook an undergraduate degree in Psychology at Liverpool University in 2004. She later completed her master's degree in Health Psychology at Liverpool John Moores University prior to undertaking a Professional Doctorate in Counselling Psychology at the University of East London.

If you've experienced difficulty in becoming pregnant or maintaining your pregnancy, Louise's new psychological approach could well hold the key to unblocking your unconscious and bringing you closer to the baby you so strongly desire.

Conceiving Conception

The Workbook

DR LOUISE GODDARD-CRAWLEY

SilverWood

Published in 2023 by SilverWood Books
SilverWood Books Ltd
14 Small Street, Bristol, BS1 1DE, United Kingdom
www.silverwoodbooks.co.uk

ISBN 978-1-80042-213-1 (paperback)

British Library Cataloguing in Publication Data

A CIP catalogue record for this book is
available from the British Library

Produced by Simon Gadd

www.conceivingconception.com

Introduction

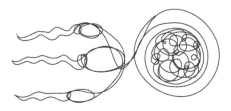

I avoided pregnancy all my life and now pregnancy avoids me.

The concept for *Conceiving Conception* arose during my ten years working as a Senior Fertility Nurse at a Harley Street clinic. During my time there I met many women grappling with infertility on both a physical and an emotional level. While the physical and biological aspects of infertility were readily tackled by the medical profession, the much more significant role that psychology played in infertility was largely ignored. The women I helped had many questions and emotions around their inability to conceive or maintain their pregnancies. It was this psychological challenge that prompted me to delve deeper into this aspect of infertility and marry the challenges of infertility with my doctorate in psychology.

After several years of working with women and couples who were unable to conceive, I came to understand that perhaps the deep psychological wiring of our brains could be linked to pregnancy. Could the brain have been affecting their ability to have a baby in ways that we may not have previously considered? Can the brain be powerful enough to affect something as biological as infertility?

The brain's ability to affect the body is well known. In recent years, countless studies have focused on stress and its direct physical effects on the person experiencing it. A quick Google search for 'stress symptoms' will bring up masses of information. Commonly documented physical side effects include: low energy, headaches, constipation, nausea, aches and pains, tense muscles, chest pain, rapid heartbeat, insomnia, frequent colds and infections, nervousness and shaking, ringing in the ears, cold or sweaty hands and feet, dry mouth and difficulty swallowing, clenched jaw and grinding teeth. Stress has even been shown to affect your cycle and ovulation – your body responds to stress and determines that now is not a good time to be pregnant.

The list is pretty long, but what is unquestionable is that stress starts in the brain. We know that psychology affects other conditions and we also know that there are huge gaps in our knowledge of neuroscience. As a result of working with many women, I believe that, as well as our brains being impacted by infertility (emotionally), the brain could also be the *source* of the infertility.

So, given what we understand about stress, is it beyond belief that in the same way as stress starts in the brain and affects the body, infertility (either without a biological cause or medically unknown) could similarly start in the brain and actively block you either from conceiving or carrying your baby to term?

I went on to complete my doctoral thesis on the subjective experience of medically unexplained infertility (MUI). My studies and subsequent practice have placed me in a unique position to help women who are involuntarily childless for reasons that are unexplained. It's my firm belief that if we can achieve a change in the way you think, in your beliefs toward pregnancy and childbirth at a much deeper level than simply saying "I want to be pregnant", we stand a chance. In fact, I have seen – first-hand and with many women – the transformations that can take place.

How many times have you heard the brain referred to as a 'muscle'? Through the exercises I have brought together in this companion workbook, I truly believe there is a way that we can retrain your brain. Your mental muscle – your deepest thoughts – can be taught to actively welcome pregnancy and, in turn, pave the way to updating your mindset to one which will help you achieve the family you desire. It's all about getting you to conceive conception deep within your brain, as well as perhaps challenging some outdated beliefs that you may unconsciously still be holding on to.

Here's an example. Since becoming sexually active, you've probably been doing pretty much anything to avoid getting pregnant. You've conditioned your brain to reject the mere thought of it. Over time, your desire not to become pregnant has had a cumulative effect which has caused your brain to continually programme your body to resist pregnancy. For the greater part of your life to date, the thought of becoming pregnant was 'bad' and you took all steps to avoid it. Now, in a relative instant, you find yourself with a burning desire to become pregnant. This 180-degree shift in thinking cannot hope to rewire decades of conscious and unconscious pregnancy avoidance like the flicking of a switch.

Over the years I worked at the clinic, what really surprised me was that my colleagues and I shared an uncanny intuition: we were able to accurately predict which patients would be successful in a fertility treatment. These predictions had little foundation in their medical history or in the way a patient presented for treatment. Often it had little correlation with how they built relationships with clinical staff. Instead, it was more aligned with an instinct/intuition. This instinct was intriguing, especially when a patient who responded well to treatment and fertilised eggs successfully still did not get pregnant. What lay behind the collective intuition? This made me curious to understand what else may be going on.

While I was still working as a fertility nurse, I started working as a trainee psychologist. Coincidentally, as a part of my training, I counselled three patients with infertility. I found the reasons these women believed they were unable to conceive extremely interesting. One of them had been told by her mother that she "wasn't wanted", and as a result was wrestling with whether she would want *her* baby once it was born. Another had had a termination in her late teens which she had kept secret from her partner and her parents. Because of this, she felt that she didn't 'deserve' to be pregnant. The third had had an uneventful first pregnancy but her labour was extremely traumatic. She lost a significant amount of blood, which saw both her and the baby perilously close to losing their lives. When she later decided to try for a second baby, she simply couldn't conceive. She was crushingly anxious about going through the trauma of delivery again, and this was holding her back. In effect, she was suffering from post-traumatic stress. Here was a woman who had previously had no issue in conceiving and carrying her baby to term but was now battling with secondary infertility.

Was there something going on at a much deeper psychological level that, in some way, connected all three women? Were they all, in a way, subconsciously sending the brain negative messages relating to pregnancy? Since qualifying and starting my own private practice, I have noticed how this pattern is pervasive. With all the women I help, there seems to be an underlying, unresolved area in their lives. This unresolved element needs to be acknowledged; it needs to be processed and it needs to be moved aside to, in effect, 'make way' for their baby.

Without exception, all of the women I've helped found that the absence of a reason for their infertility resulted in a powerful desire to find an answer. You, like these and so many other women I have counselled, have many questions. "Why can't I just get pregnant? What's wrong with me? Why do I repeatedly miscarry? Have I done something wrong? Am I a failure? Do I deserve to be a mother?" Right now I have to tell you that there is nothing 'wrong' with you. You're seeking answers to some very deep questions. I believe the answers lie in your subconscious and your mindset. At this stage, all I ask is that you remain curious and open to the concepts I will introduce. I cannot stress this enough: although I am suggesting deep, subconscious reasons for your infertility, this is not about blame. It is about working through those problems in order to make way for conception.

Recently there has been a growing awareness in people's beliefs about the causes of illness. We see an increasing concern that people's everyday understandings of illness are being silenced by 'big pharma': "just take this pill and you'll be fine". There has also been a shift of opinion around the emotional aspects of infertility. There is a growing sense that, given there is so much we don't fully understand about the brain, what goes on up there could hold the key to unlocking our unexplained infertility, especially when conventional medicine cannot explain it. My position is that anyone experiencing infertility is not intrinsically 'unwell'. What's central to all of this is your understanding and your beliefs about why you are experiencing unexplained infertility. My role is to help you overcome your difficulty in conceiving and carrying your baby to term through unlocking and understanding your brain's power.

It may be that you believe there isn't anything holding you back from becoming pregnant, or perhaps it's just something that the medical profession hasn't found yet. Please hear me again when I say that this is absolutely not about blame. This is about trying to unlock something that you may not have even thought about. Critical here is the understanding that your conscious brain (your waking thoughts) is just the tip of the iceberg. Your subconscious brain is vastly bigger beneath the surface. Throughout this book the terms 'subconscious' and 'unconscious' will be used interchangeably. They both focus on what is out of the control of our consciousness. What might have built up over time, and what might have been ingrained into your subconscious brain, that may now be standing in the way of your fertility? If we do identify and resolve something, it's critical that you don't blame yourself for this. What has built up in your brain is an effect of your subconscious. The subconscious, by its very definition, is not something we naturally focus on. You can't be held hostage by the realisation that something may have built up to hinder your fertility. What's important is that we work together to address it now.

Over the years, my patients have learned that not only do I bring my professional expertise and experience to this journey, but I am also as committed as they are to the achievement of their goals. By working through this book, not only will you gain an appreciation of the psychological challenges of Medically Unexplained Infertility (MUI), but you will also benefit from the exercises I have prescribed to help with unblocking a psychological pathway to a successful pregnancy.

You may be tempted to skip a chapter because your immediate reaction is that it's "not relevant to me". Please don't. The fact that your instinct is to resist that topic could well be an indicator of its importance. The chapter you skip could well be the one that holds the key. Your immediate reaction to the topic of a chapter may speak volumes that you don't yet fully appreciate. What we're trying to do is to make you take a step back and ask yourself why you are reacting in that way. Focus on your feelings and reactions to these chapters and we will be making progress.

This book is a step-by-step guide to psychological change and growth; these are the steps that I have shared with all my patients on their way to the formation of their new families. Together we will unlock what is happening in your brain that could be standing in the way of you having a baby. Calling on my real-world clinical experiences and examples with others who have walked the same path as you, we will work through a number of exercises. Some of these you can do on your own, some with your partner, some maybe even with friends or others you know who may be going through the same thing.

Often I reflect on the familiar echoes of my infertility patients and I recall a phrase that has been repeated time and time again, in moments of light-heartedness as well as moments of anguish: "I have spent most of my life trying not to get pregnant! And now I can't." While my job as a Harley Street fertility nurse was extremely rewarding, I also witnessed the pain and suffering associated with the inability to conceive or maintain a pregnancy. The feelings of guilt, worthlessness and self-blame were something I frequently saw my patients battling with. These sentiments were the driving force for me to bring this companion workbook to life. I've helped these women and now I want to help you. The path from pre-conception to conception and birth is a rewarding and challenging journey. This is going to take effort, and I should caution you it will be an emotional ride, but the reward at the end is the ultimate one.

Let's begin.

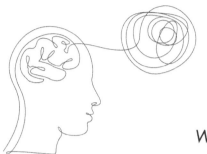

Chapter 1

When Nothing's Wrong but it Isn't Right

Well, here we are – the 'I' word. You know that infertility affects millions of people around the world. You know you're not alone in dealing with it, but it may well feel like you are. This is because your experience of infertility will not be the same as someone else's. You'll have your own stories and, although there are some common experiences, your experience of infertility is very much your own. As we get going in this chapter, I think it's right that I ask you the same first question I ask everyone I meet as they start therapy for infertility:

What does having a baby mean to you?

It's a question that you may not have been asked before. Your journey through infertility until this point has probably focused purely on causes and solutions: why can't you get pregnant? What treatments can you try to improve your chances of conceiving? The list goes on.

Infertility is defined as 'the inability to naturally conceive, carry or deliver a healthy child' (usually after one year of trying). But what this simple definition fails to recognise is the psychological fallout that people experience when they find themselves infertile. Infertility can feel like a uniquely stressful situation which is difficult to comprehend, as it's one that people rarely expect to have to deal with and one that is difficult to prepare for.

As I said, infertility affects everyone differently. I want us to try to hold on to this thought as we consider infertility more widely. I want to underline the fact that I completely understand that your experience of infertility is your own. Naturally, there will be characteristics of your experience that are very similar to others, but this is about you. I want to assure you that I won't forget that.

What is infertility?

There may seem little point in going through a brief history of infertility. You know everything there is to know about it already, right? You'll be relieved to hear that, unlike other books on the subject, I'm not going to spend a great deal of time dragging up the history of infertility. History is just that – history. It's not that relevant to you right now. What I am going to do, however, is consider the effects that infertility has on you from an emotional, physical, societal and, most importantly, psychological perspective. While I'm sure you know and have experienced a lot around this subject (you're here reading this workbook, after all), I find it helpful to frame what you're going through more broadly. It's good to take a step back and look at how it affects you, how your friends and family influence your experience of it, and how society more generally influences that experience. We need to bring to mind your personal experience of infertility, and it may help to overlay this with a broader view. If nothing else, it helps to show you that while everything you are going through is intensely personal to you, you're not alone on this journey. Many women and couples have gone before you and, unfortunately, many will follow.

Throughout history, people have been fascinated with the mysterious processes of the creation of life, both in humans and in nature more generally. Throughout the developed world, studies into the overall well-being of general populations regularly find that while having children doesn't necessarily make people happier or more satisfied, it does make them feel like they have more of a reason for living. While society at large appears to have moved away from the concept that a biological imperative drives us, people I meet still describe this 'driven' feeling very strongly. We could say that in general, for most people, having children is just a part of life. Similarly, we also see an increasing openness around *not* wanting children. We recognise that not all childless women are infertile – for some it is a choice, and it's a choice that we recognise and respect. Yet we can safely assume that if you are reading this book, having a baby is your goal.

As we know all too well, not everyone who wants to have a child is successful. Witnessing others seemingly effortlessly falling pregnant can bring up many emotions, especially when it happens for people close to us over and over again. While we recognise that, for you, having a baby is one of the main necessities of human life, when something interferes with this you can experience something of a psychological crisis. This may well impact you, the relationship you have with yourself and, in all likelihood, your relationships with others.

Fertility in society

The psychological impact and strain that people experience around infertility have, for a long time, gone unaddressed. This strain is even more pronounced around the deeply upsetting subject of miscarriage. I believe that the trauma of miscarriage is grossly underestimated and under-recognised in our society. Very often, couples usually suffer several miscarriages before they decide to seek therapeutic help. Typically these women don't see themselves as having problems with fertility – after all, they can achieve pregnancy. However, for these women maintaining pregnancy is the issue. As you can imagine (or perhaps you already know), the joy of getting pregnant followed by the shock, the loss and the pain of a miscarriage (often more than once) is an agonising event. I'm truly sorry if this has happened to you. As I say, this is such a painful experience and it is rarely given the empathy that it deserves. It is often swept over too quickly with "Oh, this is your first pregnancy? Miscarriage is normal", "It's to be expected" or "You'll get over it". But it is an acute loss. I strongly feel that the psychological pain associated with miscarriage should not be minimised. Often women I've seen for therapy internalise these societal views and deny their own pain. Sadly, this often leads to an even more complicated grieving process. We are going to have a more in-depth look at this a little later on. For now, I just wanted to take a little time to honour the experience of miscarriage/s and to recognise the suffering associated with it.

Your experience of infertility is a multilayered and complex phenomenon – of course it is. Infertility spans the biological, emotional, physical, social, financial and psychological aspects of your life and relationships. It's a big deal! And I know how much it means to you. Unfortunately, all too often society can be insensitive. I wonder how many times you've been told to "just relax" or that "it will happen when the time is right". Sadly, that just doesn't really cut it, however well intentioned the words and advice may be. Often people say these things to try to help you to create a positive mindset, but in effect, these well-intentioned comments merely encourage you to deny how you are really feeling. We'll see why this is not helpful in the next chapter.

Is infertility becoming more common?

The clinical definition of infertility is simply 'when a woman cannot conceive (get pregnant) despite having regular unprotected vaginal intercourse, or artificial insemination, at and around the time of ovulation' Biologically, falling pregnant is actually a challenging process for us all. When you stop and think about it, there is a very short window in your menstrual cycle during which conception is possible. Imagine trying to throw a ball through the open window of a passing car – you're going to fail more times than you succeed. When all is said and done, your chance of falling pregnant each month is just 25%. So, conversely, you have a 75% chance of *not* falling pregnant. This is when everything is working as expected. If there are any underlying factors that have not yet been revealed, these may be further reducing your chances. That car is moving even faster!

After a reasonable time of not falling pregnant, it's only natural that you will consider some sort of formal investigation. This train of thought is entirely justified and may well lead to a possible plan of medical treatment. In the developed world, the main categories of infertility are: ovulatory disorders (including tubal damage), which account for around 25% of infertilities; uterine or peritoneal disorders, which are said to explain 15%; and male infertility, which is thought to account for around 35%. MUI, where there is no identified male or female cause, accounts for the remaining 25% of infertilities. That means that for one in four couples suffering from infertility, a cause cannot be identified.

In the developed world, the statistics show that infertility affects one in seven heterosexual couples. This isn't to say that this demographic is our only focus, but it highlights the pervasive nature of what we are dealing with here. At the time of writing, it is further estimated that infertility affects (depending on where you look) an average 117 million people worldwide every year. Sadly, this number is on an upward trajectory. As you can see, it's more common than you may have imagined.

When you scratch beneath the surface, almost everyone knows someone else who has struggled with infertility. It is this prevalence that became the driving force behind my desire to help.

Why do more couples leave it later to start a family?

Not so very long ago, most women were starting families at around eighteen (sometimes even earlier than that). If you go further back, historic records show that girls may have started having babies as soon as they got their periods. At that time, women were primarily seen as baby-making vessels. However, in the last hundred years or so we've witnessed a social desire to have more parity between men and women. We've still got a long way to go – we're certainly not there yet – but women and men are now allowed to 'compete' on a more level playing field. The concept of the family has changed.

As a result of our more enlightened times, it has become something of a social norm that more and more women delay starting a family in order to focus on their career. Should they run into any difficulty conceiving, the medical profession appears to act as a backup plan. This observation is supported by an emerging trend towards more women freezing their eggs in an attempt to 'beat the reproductive clock'. This assumption that we can have children later when we're ready may well be borne of seeing more and more 'poster women' having children later in life. This effect, coupled with the development of newer and more successful techniques for infertility treatment and a general increase in awareness of the available services, can lead to women delaying considering a family until much later. Again, there is no judgement here – these are perfectly understandable decisions given the more equitable world of work and society that is now available to women.

It's also perfectly possible that we may simply not meet our ideal partners until we are a little older. Maybe we have just put it out of our minds while dealing with whatever life throws at us. And there are several other areas we should consider, especially with regard to how they may affect your fertility. For example, there are increasing concerns around environmental toxins, declining health conditions, inappropriate timing of sexual intercourse and stressful lifestyles. All of these can quite reasonably be considered as contributors to infertility in both sexes.

Environmental toxins

If we consider environmental toxins, in many cases we simply don't know what we're being exposed to. Many of my patients are increasingly worried about what they are putting into their bodies, but there is also a growing awareness about the potential effects of what is put *onto* our bodies: creams, scents, make-up – frankly, everything! Unless you're prepared to go fully organic, you cannot hope to know what kinds of chemicals may have been introduced to create the products you consume or use on your body. The list of potential bad actors is endless. These days we're seeing a massive push to go fully organic to rule out as many toxins as possible, but if you overlay the general unease about food and product additives and then push yourself into a typical fertility diet, you'll find that it's very restrictive. While it could be argued that we're drifting into the realms of theory and conjecture when it comes to these environmental factors, what cannot be ignored is the fact that concerns about them come up in my therapeutic sessions with great regularity.

Health conditions and obesity

In our part of the world, we are increasingly sedentary. So often my patients will have concerns about their overall health – not just around fertility but more generally. They're conscious of just how little time they have to work on their health and fitness. We tend to lead increasingly stressful and busy lifestyles, which contributes to declining health conditions. Over the past few years we've seen something of an epidemic in cardiovascular disease and type 2 diabetes. Poor diet and lifestyle choices are leading to surging obesity and to more and more people becoming insulin-dependent. The sad reality is that if you find yourself categorised as obese, this typically means you may find yourself completely ruled out from undergoing any medically assisted fertility cycles.

Timing

You'd be staggered to hear how many times the simple evidence of inappropriate timing of sexual intercourse comes up when I start talking things through with my patients. In my experience, sexual education falls well short of giving young women the knowledge they need to help themselves when it comes to achieving pregnancy. Many women I have helped simply didn't know when they were ovulating or even when they were supposed to have sex. They just went on something of a 'hunch'. Sometimes women say to me, "I'm having my period so I can't get pregnant," but what they are often unaware of is that it may not even be a 'proper' period – it could well be an ovulation bleed or a breakthrough bleed. Some women I have helped have tried using ovulation detection kits, but what the manufacturers don't say is that these are not necessarily all that reliable. So, for many, the process of trying to conceive naturally sees more than its fair share of guesswork. This is why understanding your cycle is crucial, and I will share some helpful guidance around this later in this workbook to get you on the right track. You'll find this in Chapter 4, Exercise 5.

Work-life balance

Who among us can say we're living a totally stress-free lifestyle? Stress is part and parcel of pretty much everyone's life to varying degrees. In small doses, it's even been shown to have some benefit. A common theme with many of my patients is one of significant stress – and quite often it's unrecognised until we start to consider it consciously. For the greater part of our lives, we're working – either for someone else or for ourselves. It's only natural that we typically make work a priority – after all, it's what puts food on the table and keeps a roof over our heads. But I hear more and more about the fairy-tale 'work-life balance'. Has anyone really got this cracked? If they have, they're certainly in the minority. If you're anything like me, you know you should probably dial it back a little on the work front and take a little more time to do the things you love with family and friends. That's what we *should* be doing. We know and recognise that. But knowing it and doing something about it are two very different things. Many of my patients have very little work-life balance. Of course, we're all in the rat race to a greater or lesser extent, but when you're running at full speed all the time, it's bound to be stressful.

But what if there simply isn't anything wrong?

As I mentioned, MUI accounts for around 25% of the infertility that is seen in the developed world. This is a number that appears, sadly, to be growing. You can be diagnosed with MUI only after the common causes of infertility have been excluded using standard fertility investigations. These investigations include semen analysis, assessment of your ovulation and tests of your tubal patency (how open or unobstructed your tubes are).

The medical profession has selected these tests because they have been shown to have a definite correlation with pregnancy. So you're only going to get a diagnosis of MUI once you've undergone all these tests and none of them has shown any indications of anything out of the ordinary.

So you've seen the professionals and they're all scratching their heads. On paper there is no reason why you should not be able to conceive or carry to term. We've arrived at the point of MUI. Where do you go from here?

For many women, the impact of an MUI conclusion has a profound impact. The medical profession says you're fine – but still you're not pregnant. So what now? You certainly don't feel fine. You may have more and more questions, doubts and maybe even blame. Is it all in your head? Well, in a way I believe it is.

It is at this stage that it might help to look at the mind as well as the body. Most of the women I have helped with their infertility have come to me once they have reached an MUI conclusion. That's not to say that the strategies and techniques I have developed can *only* help those with an MUI diagnosis. Naturally, if you've discovered that you physically cannot gestate a baby for biological reasons (some women discover they have no womb, for instance) then no techniques will help. All they will do is enable you to reach resolution for all that you have been through. But again, I think it's safe to assume that if you're reading this workbook, that's not the case for you. My approach can help you if you've been unable to conceive through natural means. It can help you if you've had one or more miscarriages. It can also help you if you're undergoing in vitro fertilisation (IVF) or another associated medical intervention (or even if you're considering one).

Without exception, couples I have worked with who have been handed an MUI conclusion have experienced significant social strain. They've also had multiple unresolved issues. For some of them, these issues remained present years after a failed IVF attempt. But the most striking thing I've found with these couples is that they have all felt haunted by their inability to explain why they couldn't become pregnant – not only to others but also to themselves. I believe that it is this uncertainty that is the source of their distress.

Grappling with MUI

MUI is less tangible than, say, an ovulatory disorder or tubal dysfunction. The lack of any simple cause for their infertility leaves the unexplained unexplainable. Consider this: if you know you've got an ovulatory problem, you can say "I have a problem with my tubes" and your friends and family will readily acknowledge the tangible. "Ah yes, that's why you can't have a baby, because there is something wrong with your tubes." But what about if you find yourself having to say "I can't have a baby but no one knows why"? You can't explain the pain this causes you because, for most of your social circle, it's not definitive. It's not tangible and therefore it's not relatable. It's very hard to communicate infertility or MUI – it's just so hard to translate it. It is as C. S. Lewis describes: "it is easier to say 'My tooth is aching' than to say 'My heart is broken'."

Infertility is so much more than a medical condition. It affects how you feel about yourself, your relationships and your life. Therefore, while the cause of your infertility or MUI may remain an unsolved mystery that you and/or your partner may need to accept, the subjective experience of how this may affect you should never be ignored.

The general increase in participation of fertility treatments has raised awareness and has, as a result, inspired investigation into the psychological ramifications of infertility. This isn't to say that an assumption has been made that all humans experience the impact of infertility in the same way. Our society at large is blind to the mental suffering that you are experiencing. But the more people undergo IVF, the more we understand about the psychological impact of it. Does everyone experience grief in the same way? Does everyone experience anger in the same way? These may not be your feelings, but in my experience with MUI there does seem to be a common thread. Addressing the psychology of this is fundamental to what we will be working through together.

So what's next?

Assisted reproductive technologies are available, of course, should you have the means and the opportunity. These are methods for infertile couples to achieve a pregnancy by artificial or partially artificial intervention. The use of assisted reproductive technology has become more commonplace in developed countries, and it may well be something you're considering or even already undergoing. In some countries age is a barrier to you being offered assistance, and in some cases you may only be offered two or three attempts to conceive.

Of the different treatments available, intrauterine insemination (IUI), controlled ovarian hyperstimulation (COH) and IVF are the main approaches. By any measure, IVF is the most successful intervention for couples with MUI, but it is also the costliest. At the time of writing, according to the Human Fertilisation and Embryo Authority in the UK, MUI accounted for 43% of all IVF cycles and 20% of all Intracytoplasmic Sperm Injection (ICSI) cycles (a form of IVF where the sperm is injected directly into the egg).

IVF is not an easy option. The process can be extremely invasive and is not without considerable psychological impact. In fact, the psychological effects of undergoing IVF can be almost as significant as those of the infertility itself, as it can put immense pressure on your emotions and on your relationships. In this way, the solution may cause just as much of a psychological challenge as the problem. Unfortunately, the approach for couples with MUI can be something of a 'one size fits all'; because there is no definitive cause of your infertility, a much broader medical approach is adopted.

Many people come and work with me following multiple rounds of testing – all of which have come back as 'normal'. Often they have tried everything from nutrition to acupuncture, meditation, temperature taking and more. After years of trying to conceive naturally or through IVF, they are still either unable to fall pregnant or unable to carry a baby to term. All they are left with are many unanswered questions. And when there is no simple explanation, women typically try to fill in the blanks themselves, often with self-critical and unkind results.

Whether you're on a journey of assisted reproductive technology or not, sadly, the suffering associated with your experience of infertility remains. I'm pleased to see that we're living in an era when infertility is becoming increasingly spoken about and there is less of a taboo around the subject. But that in no way diminishes how it feels for you to experience it. We're also living at a time when the medical profession can provide a range of treatments. But sometimes, despite the best efforts of the medical profession, some women still fail to conceive or carry to term.

All the currently available medical treatments focus on the physical – on your body. And all the interventions I've outlined must completely take over your menstrual cycle in order to improve your chances of conceiving. Typically, this means shutting down your natural cycle and then replicating it through the administration of drugs. If you undergo IVF, you'll find yourself needing to self-administer injections on a daily basis. You'll also need to take multiple medications on top of the hormone injections to support any potential pregnancy. These medications include steroids, blood thinners and others – all necessary to give you the best chance of a successful IVF cycle. Whichever way you look at it, IVF is not an easy solution and has at least some psychological impact. You're putting your body through a lot.

The psychological impact of medical interventions

Medical interventions can not only be difficult to undergo but can also be disruptive. If you're called in the middle of the day and told that test results show you need to administer an injection as soon as possible, it may not be that straightforward. You may find yourself at work or away from home – just where do you go to do it? Patients of mine who are going through IVF describe to me how they have had to "put their life on hold and just go with it". At the end of the day, they're handing full control of their cycle to their physician.

All these procedures and processes also naturally introduce an element of fear. After all, you don't want to get it wrong. If you undergo IVF, you'll typically have a one-time training session showing you how to handle your daily injections yourself. But how do you know you're doing it correctly? There is always support available from your clinic but, if you need to be at work and getting on with life, this isn't always easy to access immediately. Unfortunately, the injections are also not without side effects – they are hormones, after all. The process can make you feel like you're about to have a period, with all the symptoms that go along with that. Injecting yourself on a daily basis with hormones which are synthetically derived from the urine of other, fertile women is also bound to have a psychological impact – whether conscious or not.

As you can see, IVF as a process inevitably leads to stress. When you consider the financial investment, the potential to get it wrong and the impact of a daily routine of injections and medications, you can see how this intervention can place a lot of pressure on both your body and your mind. This is compounded by the underlying worry of whether it will even work. Unfortunately, while the medical profession is expert at administering the IVF process, it is not as tuned in to its psychological impact. IVF practitioners are well aware that there *is* a psychological impact, and in many cases they will advise patients to seek some form of counselling, but psychotherapy is simply not their focus. This is where I believe I can help – whether you're already on an IVF journey or you're considering one, the techniques in this workbook will give you the very best opportunity for success.

A physical focus

But what if you choose an 'alternative' route, such as acupuncture or nutrition? These are still invasive and – in the case of nutrition – restrictive. There is also the psychological impact of wondering whether this particular treatment is going to work. Do you see a pattern emerging here? Pretty much every infertility treatment out there is focused on your physical body. The physical nature of these treatments inevitably creates stress and, in some cases, distress. But what about your mind? As we touched on in the introduction, if your brain can be affected by your body, it follows that your body can be affected by your brain.

Of course, there is the possibility that it's not that your infertility cannot be medically explained – it simply cannot be explained *yet*. While there may be no current definitive diagnosis and treatment, that does not mean it will never be treatable medically at some point in the future. This can't be ruled out, as medicine is constantly evolving and improving. In the meantime there is another approach you can try.

MUI, by its own definition, focuses on the unexplained. But let's focus for a minute on what we *do* know: we know that right now you're trying to have a baby – so far without success. If you have been through fertility treatments or have suffered one or more miscarriages, it's also likely that there has been a psychological impact. While there are plenty of unanswered questions about the nature and cause of your infertility or MUI, there seems to be no question that it causes suffering.

So this is why I asked you at the beginning of this chapter to hold in mind what pregnancy means to you. This is about you, after all. Perhaps take a moment now to think about the impact your experience with fertility has had on you to date. Remember: the focus here is you.

How has your infertility affected your relationship with your partner? How has it affected your work, your career? Has it affected your relationship with sex? If you find yourself secondarily infertile, has it affected your relationship with your first child? Your life is in something of a holding pattern while you try to work this out. Are you concerned about the passage of time? Do you feel that this is time you are wasting, that you cannot get back? These are common themes I hear, so I wonder if they resonate with you.

The problem with blame

There are numerous psychological characterisations of MUI. These can include a diminished self-esteem or feeling like a 'failure' every month when, upon the beginning of a new menstrual cycle, a woman is reminded that an opportunity has passed. Without a definitive medical explanation, women seem especially vulnerable to putting blame on themselves. "Who or what is to blame?" is the question that dominates their thoughts. Every waking hour is consumed with asking "What is wrong? It must be me..."

We could say that these thoughts and feelings are inevitable. As sentient beings, humans have an innate tendency to assign meaning, cause and blame to negative life events, even those that are largely out of their control. When there is a gap in diagnosis – a gap in understanding – there is even more of a tendency for women to blame themselves.

The features of a woman's body have long been the symbols of fertility. Your womb exists solely to carry a baby. Your vagina is there to facilitate conception and as a canal to give birth to the baby. Your breasts are there to feed the baby. Unequivocally, this is their prime function. From an evolutionary perspective, if that function were dysfunctional, infertile women would have been rejected by their group, by their tribe, as the sole purpose of their existence would be defunct.

I see a link between a woman's body as a reproductive machine and what this means in society at large. By extension, acceptance or rejection depends on the outcome of your attempts to have children. Like it or not, women are judged on whether they are attractive and whether they are good at reproducing. So a woman's body – your body – becomes the representation of fertility.

If you're undergoing some form of medical assistance, in a way you're under attack all the time – your body must undergo undeniably invasive treatments, and even then it may or may not function. You have ceded control of the decisions about this part of your body to others. In effect, the medical profession is in control – not you.

As a direct consequence of this, your self-image is diminished and disrupted and you find yourself open to the judgement of others. If all your friends and extended family have children and you don't, you may feel you are not allowed to join that 'tribe'. You are missing the prerequisite membership credentials. When infertility is unexplained, it is as though the female reproductive function becomes a purely medical phenomenon, often leading to the medical manipulation of your body. For it is you, the woman, that fertility interventions largely focus on.

Fertility envy

You may feel anger and resentment about your infertility, and these are emotions that can easily be turned in on yourself. When we envy other families, other mothers, this envy does not sit comfortably with us. We don't want to be the person who envies someone else's joy. So we don't talk about it – we suppress it. But it's important to give voice to this. This envy isn't the only thing you feel – it doesn't define you. It's just a *part* of what you feel and what you're going through. If we stand back and approach this from a place of compassion, it's easy to see that envy, along with all the other emotions, just goes to show that you're human.

Over the years of working with couples, I have witnessed the profound sense of loss infertility brings. This is also difficult to grapple with – women say to me, "I haven't lost anything! It wasn't real!" Let me tell you now, it *is* real. This sense of loss is for your wished-for child, for the disappointment you feel each month, for the dream you had of co-creating. It is real, it is hard and it often leads to feelings of isolation and sadness. Stress, depression and anxiety are common consequences of infertility, stress being the most striking. It could easily be argued that with MUI it is the ambiguity that is at the root of the distress. For many, the stress connected to their inability to conceive is similar to the stress experienced by cancer or coronary heart disease patients – it is rooted in fear, uncertainty and grief.

Infertility in culture

We must also consider cultural influences on your experience, here as with all human health and reproductive behaviours. Infertility is not only a phenomenon of biology; it draws into question a perceived truth about the representations of femininity and masculinity prevailing in our culture. A great part of the stigma associated with infertility stems from our system of organised beliefs and values. These beliefs have special relevance to issues of parenthood, fertility and sexuality. The fragile balance between what you need and what society accepts can have a profound impact on your personality, your coping, your well-being and your sexual behaviour.

In my experience, the narratives of infertile patients echo the fact that women face profound social pressure to define themselves as 'successful childbearing objects'. Because our society is so crushingly pro-natalist, pro-natal or pro-baby, they feel compelled to define themselves as failures if they do not conceive. Our society embraces and reinforces the idea that parenthood and raising children should be the central focus of every person's adult life.

Pro-natalism is a strong social force. How many times have you been asked, "When are you going to get going, then?" or told "You should really be getting on with it now". Have you been on the receiving end of similar questions? It's as though today there are no social boundaries around this type of intrusive questioning. For many women, the experience of infertility in a pro-natalist culture is brutal.

If we think about fertility in these terms, we can see common threads. Those, like you, who are experiencing infertility are not 'ill' or noticeably disabled, but are indeed afflicted by a condition that prevents full participation in the cycle of life. Yet, to date, the treatment for this is biological and medical only – it is body-centric and invasive, and the chances of success are slim. You're having to deal not only with the blow inflicted by infertility to your sense of self, but also with the difficulties of presenting a simple and coherent life story to the social world in which you live.

What does having a baby mean to you?

Reading about the impacts of infertility above – although you know them all too well – might be a hard thing to do. But it's important to voice and understand them, and it's why I asked you to hold in mind what having a baby means to you. I wanted you to think about how your journey with infertility has affected you and those around you. What is your story? I invite you to have a think about that.

Right now you will most likely feel somewhat defined by your infertility. Many women in the same position do. As we work together through this workbook, we will use the knowledge that we have uncovered here as a foundation to build upon. We will work on unearthing your own experiences and begin thinking about how to effect a change in your mindset – a change that will, I'm confident, help in clearing the way to the outcome you desire so much.

We've seen how all the conventional solutions to infertility are focused on your body. Even if you haven't undergone any medical interventions yet, you also may have focused only on the physical. That's natural – those are the things that seem the easiest for you to address. You may have tracked your ovulation meticulously, considered limiting toxins or changed your diet. You may be looking at medical or alternative interventions. But not one of these interventions considers the power of your brain. When we acknowledge that the implications of infertility are deeply psychological, we must now look at whether the causes and the solutions could equally be deeply psychological. In the next chapter let's visit the final place there is left to look: your mind.

Chapter 2

*Infertility and the Mind:
Your Body Remembers*

> I believe that until your subconscious and conscious minds become
> linked, the subconscious will direct your life and you will find
> yourself repeating patterns that will feel out of your control.

In this chapter I want to start getting you to build a framework of
understanding. A framework is just that – a support system that all our
work will be based on. Building an understanding of how the mind works
will allow us to cultivate an 'authentic mindset'. By this I mean that the
way we think in our conscious mind is aligned with what's going on in
our subconscious mind – in other words, our conscious and subconscious
are no longer in conflict.

I know you're keen to get going, to get to the good stuff, but
I believe it's important that we look a little deeper into the connection
between your body and your mind so you can see how this can affect
your mindset. This is where we're going to make the most progress, as
your mindset is critical. To get you going, I need to share with you what's
going on in my mind and in the minds of the scientists and psychologists
that have brought us to this point.

The approach I'm going to teach you takes elements from fertility
counselling evolution over the last few decades and brings them all
together in concert with mind–body medicine to get to the outcome

you and I both want for you. It's only by taking a deeper, more detailed and holistic approach to your mind and shifting your focus away from any physical interventions that we will be truly successful. This is not to say that you should stop any physical interventions you are currently undertaking; I just need to shift your mind away from these and bring into focus the tools you already have access to. Physical interventions have their place, but it is your mind that holds the key.

Infertility is more than a medical condition to be treated physically or with drugs. Unfortunately, MUI seems to be exclusively treated as such. What is often overlooked is how it affects the way you feel about yourself, your relationships and your perspective on life. Inevitably, it affects the way you think you are perceived by others. Fortunately, psychological interventions, especially those emphasising stress management and coping skills, have been shown to have beneficial effects for infertility patients. This is something that both the psychological and infertility communities agree upon.

Therapy for infertility has historically been applied whenever there was a negative outcome, when individuals didn't appear to be 'coping' with a medical intervention or when they had suffered a miscarriage. My belief is that if you've been trying unsuccessfully – whether you're yet to try IVF, are going through it or have had unsuccessful rounds – there is a huge amount that remains unaddressed in your mind that could be blocking your ability to conceive or carry to term. In my opinion, fertility therapy is more than just support for people who are not coping with the effects of infertility. It can be used as a pre-emptive intervention in place of, or in conjunction with, physical interventions to increase the chances of success.

Let's take a glance back at the history of the psychological approach to fertility and why I am suggesting this innovative solution.

The mind–body connection: a history

The 1930s was, arguably, the point at which the fields of fertility and psychology started to meet. It was at this time that scientists started to think there could be an interaction between the mind and the body, and that psychosomatic medicine may have a role to play in treating certain conditions. Alongside psychosomatic medicine was psychodynamic medicine, which, in its broadest sense, was an approach to psychology that studied how your behaviour, feelings and emotions today may relate to your early experiences. In short, psychologists were making this important mind–body connection.

Regrettably, after the 1930s the medical profession moved away from this approach. The reasons for this are unclear, but I assume that the lack of empirical evidence had a part to play. Because this psychological approach was so hard (perhaps impossible) to measure, patients who were told that their physical symptoms had a psychological cause may have perceived this to mean the apportioning of blame. Although this couldn't be further from the truth, this would have been considered a damaging form of treatment for those patients.

Fast forward to today and, having recently published an article highlighting how stress can impact infertility, I found that one or two academics who were shackled to empirical evidence were quick to pour cold water on the idea. They too were at pains to caution about asserting blame. But the hard truth is that if we sidestep this approach because we're worried about raising feelings of blame (implied or assumed), we would be doing you a great disservice. In other words, unless you can make your way past any thoughts of blame, you won't progress. Without adopting a more open-minded approach, we risk missing the most valuable insights. My approach is not about blaming you for things that may have happened in your past. It's about owning things that may well have been out of your control and reframing and reprocessing them.

Over the years, clinics offering medical interventions such as IVF have started to recognise that supporting the mind helps to support the body and, by extension, the treatment. Sadly, they still only apply psychological approaches to support those with negative outcomes. It's never occurred to them that the cause of infertility may be psychological. This is the area of infertility I am seeking to radically change.

The methods in this book need to be applied as soon as possible when trying to achieve pregnancy. As you will come to understand, any unresolved parts of your past could well hamper your efforts at becoming and staying pregnant. My belief is that it's better to begin addressing anything that may stand in your way at the earliest opportunity. In many ways, the work we will do in this book will help you at a more holistic level regarding your general mental health. By adopting my techniques, any mental blocks can be identified and 'treated' prior to conception; or, at the very least, the heartache associated with unsuccessfully trying can be recognised with respect and compassion.

So I'd like you to start to look at your infertility the other way around. If physical infertility affects you psychologically, then perhaps the reverse path holds true as well. Any anxiety you may be feeling may not simply be the result of your infertility; it could well be a cause too. Put simply, there may have been events and beliefs in your life that need to be brought from the unconscious into your conscious mind. The processing of these events will, I believe, pave the way to creating the most helpful mindset when trying to have a baby. I call this your authentic mindset. This mindset is crucial to achieving the outcome you desire so very strongly. But just how do we get to that part of your unconscious mind?

Getting to the source of the issue

Accessing your unconscious mind is easier said than done. In the early 1950s a group of psychiatrists, including Humphry Osmond and John Smythies, experimented with the use of psychedelic drugs to access the subconscious. They found that psychedelics (especially MDMA, mushrooms and ayahuasca) dampened down the amygdala, which is the part of the brain that controls the 'fear' emotion. Once the patient became fearless, they could talk about traumatic events without retraumatising themselves.

I'm not suggesting you take hallucinogenic drugs to access your unconscious mind. But this is what I try to replicate in a therapeutic setting and what I will try to replicate here with you.

Using the coming activities and exercises, we're going to try to get through to this hidden part of your brain by removing fear and shame so that you can access your subconscious. Instead of psychedelic drugs, we'll get there through the use of creativity, imagination and curiosity.

If we consider the aim of both approaches (the use of psychedelics and my clinical verbal approach), they both seek to do the same thing: to access the consciously inaccessible. By accessing this part of your mind, if you're suffering with unexplained infertility we may find something there that needs to be examined.

Here's an example of what I mean. I once treated a patient we'll call Bella, who was thirty years old and very successful in the corporate world. While she was not suffering with infertility, she came to me when her father died and she was finding it difficult to cope. She simply could not stop crying, and was struggling to function. By working together we were able to resolve some of her grief, but I found that her symptoms – which included anxiety, regular night terrors and tension in her jaw and hands – persisted.

We concluded that while the death of her father was the immediate trigger for her coming to me for therapy, the anxiety she was feeling came not from the death of her father but from something else that had simply been masked by her grief. In other words, the cause of her anxiety that I was trying to reach lay beneath her immediate feelings.

Once we had worked through Bella's grief, I was able to approach her anxiety from a different perspective. To re-analyse her anxiety I asked her to tell me everything that she knew about the time of her conception – everything she knew about her mother's experience of pregnancy and what was happening at the time she was born. It transpired that her mother was pregnant with her during the Communist invasion and occupation of Poland. Her parents' lives were full of uncertainty and danger, and her mother was frequently hiding, running and living in fear. Naturally, her mother was in a constant state of stress during her pregnancy. When Bella was born the family was still under threat, and as a toddler she began to have night terrors. She would wake up in the middle of the night screaming, her hands adopting a clawlike position. Bella had lived with this ailment ever since, and during her teens several surgical opinions had been sought, all of which were inconclusive.

As you can see, Bella's was a very deeply set trauma that had developed before she even had the words to articulate or understand what she had experienced *in utero* and following her birth. The stress hormones from her mother would have been coursing through her in the womb, but she couldn't put her trauma into words because it was so early in her life. It was a bodily memory, not a mind memory – her body remembered it in her jaw and hands and in her unconscious anxiety. It was only by accessing this trauma that Bella was eventually able to heal.

I feel confident that even in less extreme situations, we will be able to access your unconscious through the exercises in this book. But before we tackle these, let's look at some of the emerging theories that have more recently come to light.

How the mind impacts the body

Over the last few decades, fascinating insights have been made into the link between neuroscience and the immune system. The most recent work around this subject was conducted by Dr Robert Adler and led to the field of psychoneuroimmunology (PNI). PNI is simply the study of mind–body medicine. The main thrust of PNI is that the state of someone's mind can have a profound impact on their immune system – either in a positive or a negative way.

PNI can be broken down like this:

Psycho = what you are thinking and feeling
Neuro = your brain and nervous system functions
Immunology = your body's immune responses and workings

In other words, PNI looks at the interactions between your central nervous system and your immune system. Researchers know that our central nervous system and immune system can communicate with each other, but they have only recently started to understand how they do it and what it means for our health and well-being.

What's so interesting about PNI is that it shows that what is happening in your mind can literally cause inflammation in your body and affect your immune system. PNI has deep ramifications for the future of medical research, the treatment of diseases and our attitude toward handling stress – and, crucially, I believe it has a role to play in your fertility. What might have been referred to as pseudoscience a few decades ago now finds strong support from many quarters. Let's take a closer look at how PNI can be used to heal physical and psychological conditions.

PNI and bereavement

We've all heard stories of recently bereaved individuals dying soon after their partner, especially among older adults. These tales are not just anecdotal. One study of nearly 100,000 elderly people found that those who had recently lost their partner were more than twice as likely to die in the year following their partner's death. Clearly there is more to this than a metaphorical 'broken heart'.

PNI and skin complaints

Eczema, psoriasis and even asthma are all known to have psychological aspects to them, and many sufferers will know that a stressful day at the office can exacerbate symptoms.

PNI and wound healing

There appears to be a clear link between mindset and how quickly someone heals following surgery. People who experience increased levels of fear or distress before surgery are more likely to be associated with worse clinical results. These can include complications following surgery, needing to spend longer in hospital than similarly afflicted patients and an increased likelihood to need a return visit or readmission to hospital. One study carried out on patients with severe leg wounds found that those with high levels of anxiety and depression were significantly delayed in terms of their wound healing.

PNI and HIV (human immunodeficiency virus)

There is also much evidence to support the assertion that raised stress levels combined with a lack of support from friends and family will accelerate someone's rate of decline following the detection of an HIV infection. Everyone needs a social support network, and one of the first questions I ask my patients when we start therapy is: "Who knows you are coming to therapy?"

PNI and cancer

Any health professional working with cancer patients will tell you that a patient's outlook often affects the outcome of their disease. It seems that the beliefs the patient has about their diagnosis – positive or negative – have a direct effect on their outcome. What's critical here is that I am not talking about a simple denial or acceptance of the facts but about the 'truth' that the person holds inside their subconscious – their deeply held beliefs. This is where having an authentic and aligned mindset comes in.

PNI and the gut

It is now well established that there is a strong association between sustained stressful life events and the gut. You may well have experienced this yourself. Stress can instigate and accelerate the onset of symptoms in functional gastrointestinal disorders, inflammatory bowel disease and irritable bowel syndrome (IBS). How many times in life have you noticed your own 'gut reaction' to stress or perhaps something that may be causing you anxiety – a presentation at work, relationships or a stressful home life? How often have you felt your stomach 'drop' if you've heard bad news?

So it's widely recognised that psychological stress causes immune problems: stress triggers inflammation and suppresses your immune function. But what does your immune function have to do with infertility?

Under normal circumstances, your immune system changes substantially to support a healthy pregnancy. Your body will exhibit lowered inflammatory responses and immunity so as to protect your foetus from rejection by your own immune system. In IVF, specific medication is administered to lower immune responses to mimic the body's natural behaviour. My therapeutic approach is aimed at reducing your immune response levels without medication, and one of the ways we do this is to deal with stress.

In the 1980s neuroscientist Dr Candace Pert discovered what is known as the opiate receptor – the part of your brain's cells that allows for the binding of endorphins. She considered these interconnected receptors to be the 'Molecules of Emotion', as they produce feelings of bliss, hunger, anger, relaxation or satiety. Her firmly held belief was that our body is the physical manifestation of our subconscious mind. Let that sink in for a second, as it is central to the learning we are doing in this chapter. It means that what is going on in your subconscious mind is being manifested by your body. This ties in with the overall

PNI approach and the approach that you and I are going to work on together. Fundamentally, the state of your mind has a direct effect on your immune system, health and well-being. When things go wrong in any part of this intricate and interconnected system, it may be reflected by the other parts. This can become a vicious cycle of decline in function and efficiency; but equally, as soon as a positive change occurs, the whole system improves as it wants to run at peak performance. We need to create some upward momentum in your interconnected system.

Positive mindset vs authentic mindset

For a long time there's been a feeling that a positive outlook on life – having a cheery disposition – might help you to stay healthy. In the past this was dismissed as something of a fable. But what if it isn't? The link between the mind and the immune system might seem tenuous, but it's now a fully interdisciplinary area of study. Until now it hasn't played a role in infertility, but this is where I am asking you to make an intuitive leap with me with regard to your unexplained infertility.

Most people know that stress can induce illness and that, conversely, a fun-filled occasion with loved ones can soothe aches and pains. As they say, laughter is the best medicine. Sound a bit over-simplistic? I'm not for one moment suggesting that you can laugh your way to pregnancy, but if we can dispel or dilute whatever may have caused you distress in the past or present or may perhaps even be causing a fear for the future, it can clear a way for your unconscious mind to catch up with the conscious one – the one that wants you to become a parent.

Let me be clear: I'm not telling you that a positive mindset will get you pregnant. Rather, what we need is an authentic mindset – a mindset where the unconscious and conscious minds are no longer in conflict. Conflict, as we know and appreciate, creates stress. So our goal is to align both parts of your mind to clear a path to an authentic mindset and onward towards your baby.

It is readily acknowledged by the medical community that stress-induced immune problems during pregnancy have unique implications for both your health and that of your baby. To me, the reverse of this link is crystal clear: any stress, any unconscious anxieties, anything that is not fully processed or 'worked through' psychologically can have an impact on the function of your body *before* you get pregnant.

The mind is the key

It may come as a shock to hear this, but infertility – your infertility – can be classified as an autoimmune disease. And there is a body of evidence to suggest – and it is my belief – that autoimmune diseases have their origin in the mind and later take shape in the body. Some argue that they result from an essential inability to verbalise emotions, while others believe that they are a defensive response to emotional dysregulation. Other theories categorise them as body delirium which stems from depression or as a response to an unresolved conflict. Either way, let's (continue to?) work together to unravel what's going on in your mind and identify some potential root causes.

Whatever the argument, belief or theory, every unexplained infertility patient I have treated points to the same thing: that there is something in their unconscious mind that holds the key to unlocking their chances of having a baby. My job is to help you understand this in the same way and then, through understanding it, to shift your mindset in a way that helps us to tackle it.

Let's consider the array of widely recognised autoimmune diseases. These include multiple sclerosis, psoriasis, arthritis, insulin-dependent diabetes, lupus, IBS, chronic fatigue syndrome and a host of other disorders. So far, the symptoms and development of these illnesses are known but – essentially – what triggers them is still uncertain. What we do know is that these conditions all arise when there is an overactive immune system. We also know that the mind plays an important role in all these diseases. If the psychosomatic approach or PNI hypothesis is rejected, human autoimmune diseases remain a medical and scientific mystery. Now, here's the connection I need you to make: your mind and mindset play a crucial role in your infertility.

The body is remembering

In the early twentieth century, well-known psychologists such as Freud became deeply interested in research around the ability to treat physical disorders through working with a patient's mind. If we look at his early theories of hysteria, he was hinting towards a mind–body connection, and although his hysteria theory is now rejected, it seems as though he may have been onto something. So let's take a look at a few illustrative examples that show exactly what this all means and how the same principles could be used to help you.

After World War One, many soldiers suffered from what was then called 'shell shock'. There are many films of soldiers not being able to walk on their return from the war, or with constantly shaking bodies. The things they had experienced and witnessed were manifesting physically because they were too much for the brain to cope with. We now know this to be post-traumatic stress disorder (PTSD) – the body remembering trauma.

The brain's defence mechanisms push these experiences into the body because it's 'safer' there than in the brain. These are known as 'somatoform disorders'. By pushing it into the body, the person doesn't have to relive the trauma in their mind; they don't have to keep traumatising themselves. But the experience still stays in the body and causes the body to behave in an irregular way. The solution is to pull this trauma from the body back to the mind in a conscious way. Then, once we're holding it in our mind and not our body, the body becomes free to behave in the way it should.

A good example of this somatoform behaviour is a patient we'll call Ben, whom I was treating for erectile dysfunction. Yes, there was something wrong with his body – it wasn't functioning in the way that it should – but there was nothing medically 'wrong' that was causing the condition. It was all social anxiety and pressure: because it had happened to him once, he kept thinking it would happen to him all the time. It became a self-fulfilling prophecy.

As we worked backwards through Ben's life, we discovered that his problem had started when he was eighteen and his (then) serious girlfriend abruptly ended their relationship when she left to go to university. They had also just gone through a termination together. At the same time, all his friends deserted him – they simply turned against him, and he never worked out why. This episode in his life was so traumatic for his adolescent mind that for six months he simply lay in bed, unable to function. Once he managed to get himself together and was able to get out of bed, he never talked about it.

About ten years later the erectile dysfunction happened when he began a more serious relationship once more. Ben's body remembered the trauma of the previous break-up and this triggered the physical condition as a way of protecting him – either from engaging in another relationship where he risked being hurt again or from the feelings around the unwanted pregnancy in his teens.

Ben and I worked through an exercise I am going to show you later in this workbook. I asked him to personify the fear and anxiety he felt when he went into a sexual situation. At this stage, he was so upset by everything that he decided to personify it as the Devil. We worked together to process his powerful emotions around anger and guilt, and transferred them to the Devil. The idea of the Devil became a conduit for releasing him from these emotions and transferring them out of his body.

While this process took place over several sessions, the majority of the sessions I had with Ben were focused on working out what his initial trauma was – we had to work backwards. Importantly, his story shows that sometimes a normal function of the human body fails to work because it has been interrupted by an emotional trauma. When we connected Ben's conscious mind back to a prior trauma and processed that through the techniques we will be using in this workbook, normal service was restored.

When we think about unexplained infertility, does this story sound familiar? There is nothing 'medically' wrong with you, but something's not right. Ben was suffering from performance anxiety – in other words, it was all in his head – but that doesn't mean we can dismiss it, as the symptoms are real. It shows without doubt that the mind plays an integral role in the functioning of our bodies.

If you have experienced trauma and it's been severe, your body will remember it even if your mind does not. I say this because I have seen it countless times – what's going on in your mind holds the key to the healing of your body. Everyone's body keeps a record.

When biology has no explanation, where does that leave you?
Health can't always be understood by biology and medicine. After all, I see you as much more than just pathologies. Who we are as individuals,

including our psychological, social and cultural variables, will affect how our health is experienced subjectively.

It's not uncommon to hear of couples going through IVF who, as soon as they stop trying, fall pregnant. The moment they resign themselves to the fact that it's not going to happen, they release the pressure on themselves and the natural process takes over. The fact that they had stopped consciously trying may mean something. Now, I am not able to account for how or why this occurs, but it does – which means there is something happening at a psychological level. It means there is a psychological factor that we need to consider when it comes to MUI. Once they stop trying, these couples experience a fundamental shift in mindset. It's this move towards an authentic mindset that this companion workbook will empower you to experience.

Bringing it all back to you

So let's consider your situation. You're suffering with unexplained infertility or the inability to carry your baby for the full term. With no obvious medical cause, psychological causes must be considered. As we've said, you've already tried everything else, right? So what's going on in your mind?

In my experience, there doesn't seem to be a particular psychological profile associated with MUI. As a result, there is no specific psychological group that sees a cause and effect between the mind and the body. There is no simple 'type' of person, history or situation that leads to MUI. It's not as easy as saying, "Ah, you've experienced X – therefore if we treat Y, you'll have a baby." I wish it were that straightforward.

What is happening in your mind is, of course, unique to you. Your life story and experiences to this point are, quite naturally, deeply personal. This means that the way we approach this challenge needs to be tailored for you. Ordinarily in a one-to-one setting this is what I would do. It's challenging to recreate the same tailored approach through the medium of a book, but that is what this workbook intends to do. Together I want to explore your internal world and become curious about what may perhaps need some special attention.

44

Whatever you believe, your mind can achieve and will conceive (both figuratively and literally!)

Before we start, let's get to the source of any unconscious mental blocks. When our subconscious minds hold us back from pursuing something we desire, it's often because we may be holding a conflicting belief about it. Your mindset plays a critical role in how you cope with challenges. I believe that stress is one of the primary drivers – if not *the* primary driver – of infertility. And stress isn't just 'I have a deadline'. It comes to us in both conscious and unconscious forms.

Once we're aware of what's causing us stress, we can take action where we're able. Improving our stress levels helps us to create some resolution and, by extension, the authentic mindset we need. Becoming aware of what is causing stress is the first stage in resolving it. In short, if we feel we can do something about it, we can begin to process it and build this authentic mindset – one that's free from any unconscious anxiety. So how do we do that?

Generally, in order to process something, we construct an internal narrative. These internal stories that we tell ourselves are the foundation of our authentic mindset. Your mindset is the collection of thoughts and beliefs that shape your view of your fertility. And your mindset affects how you think, what you feel and what you do. It has an impact on how you make sense of the world and how you make sense of you.

Your mindset is a big deal.

Exercise 1: Start a gratitude journal

We all know that this journey to fertility is hard and takes its toll. To give you the best opportunity of achieving an authentic mindset, we need your mind to be in a certain state, so I want to help you shift your mindset from one of 'wanting' (your baby) toward one of 'having'. This is a mindset of being grateful for what you have instead of being focused on what you want or what you're missing. The most effective way of creating this shift is to start with gratitude. Remember, I'm not asking you to just 'be positive' in your mindset – an authentic mindset has both positives and negatives. Let's start building your authentic mindset now.

I want you to write down five things every day that you're grateful for. Please don't fall into the trap of writing down things that you have *achieved*. While they're undoubtedly important, this is not about achievements. I want you to record the things you are grateful for. They don't have to be big things either. They can be as simple as "I'm thankful for my morning cup of coffee". This is a daily practice and I'd like you to commit to it *every day*. I have made space in this workbook for you to start here, but don't stop when the page is full. Commit to this – it's important.

Notes:

....

....

....

....

....

....

....

Consolidation

This chapter has introduced and examined the concept of psychosomatic infertility and why this is not about blame. I know you're keen to get to the actionable parts of this companion workbook, so I'm glad you took the time to understand the science and thinking behind my approach. Your investment in this chapter will pay you back as we move forward. Now our job is to get the root of your mindset: your outlook. We need to understand what's led you to this point, to acknowledge it, to process it and to move you closer to your ultimate goal.

We've seen that there are realities in the minds of people that find a way of expression through disease in the body. Put simply, the state of your mind has a direct effect on your immune system, your health and your well-being. Your (unconscious) mind affects your body and, therefore, your fertility. When people come to me, they are all too often seeking my help to handle the grief and stress of their infertility. My frustration is that they are coming to me much too late. They're seeking therapy for the effect of their infertility; I want to help them with the cause – a cause which, in my understanding, has its origins in the mind.

So let's put our minds together.

Chapter 3

*Your Desire for a Baby:
Then, Now and in the Future*

In this chapter I would like us to think about your desire for pregnancy – your desire to have a baby and to start (or extend) your family. We need to take a long, hard look at this because your desire for a baby is, for the most part, a recent change in mindset. You may be thinking, "What do you mean? We've been trying for years!"

Take a moment and think about just how much of our lives we have told our brains we weren't ready for a baby.

Whether you've been trying to conceive for some time or you're just starting on the journey, the following exercises, which we will work through together, are relevant to you. But before we get into the work, let's consider why we even need to do it in the first place. I'll be using some real-world examples here to try to explain that your mindset around having a baby may be in need of an update. Having a baby may previously have been viewed as an unwelcome event. We're going to focus on and bring to the surface some deeply ingrained unconscious beliefs. We're going to do this so that I can help you to identify, and subsequently refresh, your own deeply held beliefs and desires around pregnancy and then solidify them into an updated mindset. As we work together, we will nurture some concepts that may help to unblock your unconscious mind.

But just how do you go about 'unblocking' your unconscious mind? I know what you're thinking – you haven't got a 'blockage'. Well, in a way, you might have. To figure this out, I'm going to ask you to complete several exercises as we work through this chapter. I'll also give examples of how this might look during a one-to-one therapy session. In a way, I'm coaching you to become your own therapist. This might feel a little odd at first, but I'd ask you to keep an open and creative mind. The exercises will require a little imagination, and it's very likely that they will need you to step out of your comfort zone and look inward towards yourself. I feel confident you can do this, as I know you have the desire.

So why do we need these particular exercises? Let's consider some of the typical thought patterns of people like you who are trying to conceive. While some of these examples may resonate with you, some may not. I would recommend reading all of them, however, as while these words may belong to the beliefs of others, they all point to the same thing: a deep-rooted, unconscious bias toward the belief that "pregnancy is bad". This is why it's so important that we identify your own beliefs and unblock them – to reframe them in a way that allows us to reverse these beliefs and reprogramme them. If we can reprogramme your beliefs, we can pass a new message to your unconscious mind that "pregnancy is good". And having passed that new message on, we will then work on ways to reinforce it. This ongoing reinforcement will guide you towards the right authentic mindset.

Reprocessing the past

First of all, let's take a look at what happened with a patient called Sarah. While this is not about her desire for pregnancy, it's a real eye opener about the power of 'processing' things that have happened in your past.

Sarah was a twenty-year-old Cambridge student, and I met her about a year after she had suffered two close family bereavements in quick succession. Sarah's body had shut down. She simply couldn't stop sleeping – so much so that she had almost failed her first year at Cambridge because she just couldn't get out of bed. Her symptoms of fatigue were overpowering and relentless. Working together, we identified that her trauma went way back to when, at a very young age, she was identified as a gifted child. One of her mother's 'friends' took Sarah away, moved her to another country and raised her as her own child. Sarah was literally ripped from the arms of her mother.

Sarah's new 'mother' showed psychopathic tendencies. There were two other boys with Sarah in her new family, and these boys were abused by the mother. As the special, 'gifted' one, however, Sarah was put on something of a pedestal. At the same time, Sarah was made to feel as though she was very much a burden on her foster mother. She was systematically stripped of her self-worth and self-esteem and left feeling very confused. Sarah's foster brothers were treated very poorly and considered almost "backward" by their foster mother, but anything and everything bad that happened to the family was made to be Sarah's fault.

Throughout Sarah's entire school career, right up until she went to Cambridge, she was severely bullied. Then, tragically, one of her brothers died in a car accident. A short while after that, her grandmother (to whom she was incredibly close) died. At this point it was simply all too much for Sarah and this was when her body shut down, the trauma manifesting in her body as chronic fatigue. However, contrary to the opinions of others in the medical profession who had diagnosed Sarah with chronic fatigue syndrome, I treated her for PTSD.

After six months of treatment, Sarah's fatigue was significantly diminished. How could we have achieved this remarkable turnaround in such a short space of time? We processed everything by transporting Sarah back to those troubling points in time. We spoke to the younger Sarah back then and we rationalised what was happening. We explained why these things were happening and reframed the situations and actions of others. None of it was Sarah's fault, just like your present challenge is not your fault. There were influences outside Sarah's control, just like there are influences outside your control. Sarah was a child at the time, so we needed to process what had happened to her in order for her to move on with her life in a healthy, healing way. Through doing this we were able to guide her body back to a normal level of function.

While working with Sarah, I asked her to complete several exercises where she was asked things like:

- *If you were able to talk to your younger self, what would you say?*
- *In what tone would you talk to yourself?*

- *What does that younger self need?*
- *What does she need to hear?*
- *What does she need to know about her future? That it all works out okay?*

In this way, we worked together to lay Sarah's past demons to rest. We did nothing more than simply talk and think together about the feelings and impact of these events. Talking it through was the way to 'process' what had happened. The simple action of revisiting these episodes and just talking about them was sufficient to unpick them and to reprocess them. In essence, we worked through her multiple traumas in order for her conscious mind to be better able to tolerate them through understanding. Because she'd been unable to make sense of her internal and external world, her body had attempted to protect her by storing and holding on to her multiple traumas. That's what's so exciting about what we're going to do together in this chapter. We're going to talk things through. We're going to simply make the unconscious conscious and, by extension, allow your body to function as it should.

Beliefs then and now

Let's move on now to look at a couple of examples where I have worked with women around pregnancy. Here is an exchange that took place between myself and Jo, who was suffering from unexplained infertility:

> **Louise:** *Do you remember how you felt as a teenager about getting pregnant?*
> **Jo:** *As a teenager, and in my early twenties I…for many years I didn't want children… It just wasn't on my agenda. I even remember saying to my family it was "not my thing".*
> **Louise:** *Not your thing?*
> **Jo:** *That it wasn't an option. I knew I was definitely not ready for a child at that age and, thankfully, live in a country where abortion is a possibility.*

Jo's conviction here was strong. Considering that Jo had been trying for over a year to get pregnant, it was clear that her conscious mindset for a baby had changed. But did her brain know?

Let's look at another example:

> **Maria:** *Having had it always instilled in me that I shouldn't get pregnant, it now comes as a shock to do a full 180-degree turnaround. It comes as a shock that there are now difficulties in conceiving. It's a difficult mindset.*

If we think about what Maria said here, we can see how her unconscious brain may have been given the message (or, as she said, it was 'instilled' in her) that she shouldn't get pregnant. In other words, "pregnancy is bad".

Today Maria's mindset around pregnancy has dramatically changed. This is a reflection of how, typically, our mindset around pregnancy shifts over time. The desire for pregnancy in the past is the opposite of the desire for pregnancy in the present. Maria went on to explain:

> **Maria:** *Having come from a Catholic educational background with Catholic parents, my every waking thought, like I am sure many others had at the time despite their religion, was spent trying to avoid pregnancy.*
> **Louise:** *You say despite your religion?*
> **Maria:** *Well, yes, we were told that sex was bad! Sex was dirty!*
> **Louise:** *So you avoided it?*
> **Maria:** *No, we avoided getting pregnant. Or at least tried to. We were all having sex, sort of secretly – knowing that we probably shouldn't.*
> **Louise:** *It sounds like there were some very strong beliefs about pregnancy and what you're 'supposed' to be doing?*
> **Maria:** *Yes, well, I'm sure my parents wanted to protect me. If I'd have fallen pregnant at that age it would've been a catastrophe. That's a bit strong – it would've been an unpleasant surprise.*

Now, while Jo and Maria's experiences and thoughts will likely not be exactly the same as yours, that's not the point here. What I want you to do is to begin to recognise how your early thoughts around pregnancy may well have become entrenched in your mindset. I want you to spot the signs of when your outdated notions of pregnancy may have first taken hold. Your 'Eureka' moment on this journey is when I can get you to start thinking as I do – in a more psychological way. For you to succeed, you need to get into the practice of thinking back to yourself at a point in time and interpreting what was happening then. Consider this chapter a psychological 'warm-up exercise' to get your mental agility firing.

Let's look at another example:

> **Louise:** *Can I ask you to think back to your past? What sort of beliefs did you have around pregnancy when you were younger?*
>
> **Emma:** *Yeah, I think during my teens, twenties and even now in, like, my early thirties, becoming pregnant was something to be actively avoided. Yes! I thought of it as something terrible! That should be avoided at all costs!*
>
> **Louise:** *Terrible, you say?*
>
> **Emma:** *Yes, like it was the worst thing in the world, and when it happened, it was! It was a problem to fix.*
>
> **Louise:** *What was?*
>
> **Emma:** *When I got pregnant.*
>
> **Louise:** *Is it okay to ask you more about that?*
>
> **Emma:** *Yes. I got pregnant when I was seventeen. It wasn't what I wanted, not then. I wasn't ready. I…I…um, I think the teenage me was terrified of getting pregnant. I was shocked that it happened.*

With Emma, as is quite common with many women, fear was a constant theme. Did you get that from Emma's transcript? Stop and reread the last statement – did you notice it? Her fear? Maybe you read the words but the theme of fear didn't really jump out at you.

As you've just read, when I talk with women about their early thoughts and experiences around pregnancy and they use words such as 'terrified', it suggests that there was more than just an acceptance that pregnancy wasn't for them then and that it would just happen later. The use of words such as 'terrified' points towards a conscious decision to avoid pregnancy, primarily due to its terrifying nature. This is understandable for them at that point in their lives. Feelings of fear have featured on several occasions with my patients. When you stop and think about it, could any of that resonate with you? Do you recall having similar feelings at any point in your younger years? A similar mindset? I know that when I was a teenager I felt the same. So let's see how we can process this and unblock it to get the outcomes we need.

There was, of course, a reason I chose these examples. They show that, whatever the circumstances, the message your brain gets during your formative years is that "pregnancy is bad". It's inevitable that the more we tell our brains something, the more that message – that neural pathway, that mindset – becomes ingrained. Much like learning your lines for a school show, the more you rehearse them, the more you'll be able to recall them. It's the same with your thoughts on pregnancy.

Unlearning to relearn

Think about this concept of reinforcing thoughts and beliefs much like writing, or driving, or even brushing your teeth. You've done these things so often that they are second nature. You do them now without even giving them a conscious thought. These skills and thoughts are deeply ingrained in your mind and will never be forgotten. But what happens when we ask you to write or brush your teeth with the opposite hand? What happens if we ask you to drive in a foreign country on the 'wrong' side of the road in a car with the controls on the 'wrong' side? It's not impossible, but it's certainly tricky. This is what I want you to do when it comes to your pregnancy mindset. Your mind is running on autopilot with regard to babies. It's saying, "Yep, I heard you: pregnancy is bad. I've got it, leave it to me, I'll take care of it." Now we have to switch off your mental autopilot and change to manual control. It's hard and clunky at first, but the more you do it, the better you will become.

Your unconscious thoughts around pregnancy are something that you now have to consciously 'unlearn' in order to 'relearn'. This unlearning is the tricky part. This is the part that feels awkward at first. In effect, we're working to change what *was* real to you back *then*. When we try to change your deeply held beliefs from that point in time, it's not as simple as flicking a switch. You must unlearn to relearn. That's what we're going to do in the exercises I've created for you.

It's important to point out here that we can feel differently about something on two different levels. In this case, we're talking about how you felt about pregnancy then and how that contradicts with your desire for pregnancy now. When we look at your desire for pregnancy now, you have explicit beliefs about what you desire – a baby – and how you think that may look in your mind's eye. Your beliefs are conscious, deliberately formed and easily articulated.

What I have tried to highlight is that your brain may have ingrained some implicit beliefs on an unconscious level. These beliefs have been formed in the past and no longer exist at the conscious level, which may be causing conflict with the authentic mindset we are trying to achieve. These thoughts no longer reflect what you want now, but they have already created that neural pathway. To switch it, you've got to understand the difference between beliefs and thoughts. You can't just 'think' yourself pregnant, but you can help your brain to understand what you now want.

Beliefs and thoughts

Thoughts are fleeting, whereas beliefs are much more solid – almost like a solidification or crystallisation of many years of repetitive thoughts. The more often you repeat a thought, the more solid it becomes, and eventually it transitions into a belief. Your brain will understand these implicit beliefs as a memory and will act accordingly. This is why you can't trick yourself into having a positive mindset. A genuinely authentic mindset has to be built on a solid foundation of updated beliefs.

Unless we work hard now to unblock them, your unpleasant intrinsic feelings from the past may remain, unconsciously causing less than favourable associations with a baby today. You may be automatically activating your outdated beliefs every time you consciously think of having a baby. This is why it's our job to reprogramme this. A baby is no longer something to be considered a 'bad' thing and is, instead, desired.

Here I want you to STOP and understand something critically important. In fact, it's so important that I've written it in bold:

Unless we unblock and update this belief, your brain won't know that you've made a change.

Whenever you think about babies at a conscious level, something may be unconsciously activated where your brain says, "Oh yes, you told me pregnancy is bad – got it." You want a baby but your mind may be subverting your chances without you even knowing it. This understanding of how your implicit beliefs may have adapted over time, or have perhaps remained unconscious and activated automatically, could be key to reprogramming your brain.

Let's move on now to consider your own implicit beliefs.

Often, when I'm working with someone who is trying to get pregnant or has had several miscarriages, I will ask them to spend some time thinking back to their teenage years. I want to know what experiences they may have had around pregnancy and where some implicit beliefs may have been formed. Here's an example:

Louise: *How did you get on thinking about the teenage you? Did anything come to mind? Anything that stood out as an experience where you remembered pregnancy as bad?*

Kim: *Yes, actually. I remembered being seventeen. I had been in a relationship with my boyfriend for about a year. He was much older than me, so we hid our relationship from my parents.*

Louise: *Okay.*

Kim: *We had been having sex and using contraception. Well, we had been using condoms. I…I was in love with him. But I was young and, I guess, still a little 'wild'… I was out with my friends one evening. And I slept with someone else. A boy my own age. Anyway, we didn't use protection. I had to go and get the morning-after pill. I remember freaking out that I would get pregnant. Not just in terms of the pregnancy – but that I had cheated. I remember being in the doctor's waiting room with my friend who I had made come with me. We were nervously laughing and giggling and I remember feeling so anxious about speaking to the doctor. Who was, by the way, very judgemental about it. She looked at me like I was a slut or something! Anyway, I got the pill. Walked out of her office to go and meet my friend and I remember seeing my boyfriend walk through the doors. I felt my stomach drop. He saw me, and I remember his face looking so confused about why I was there.*

Louise: *Go on.*

Kim: *I made something up. I lied to him. Like I had lied to him about the night it happened. I felt so guilty. I'll never forget that.*

Louise: *Well, there is a lot here, isn't there?*

Kim: *Yeah, there is. Also, I had been drunk when it happened with the other guy. It happened in a park. It was – well, it wasn't very sort of civilised. I look back at that and feel really ashamed. I don't even think I've talked about it since or even thought about it! But yeah, I took the morning-after pill. And my boyfriend and I broke up a few months later. But I think I didn't really forgive myself. It wasn't the same. I could tell he didn't believe me when he caught me at the doctor's.*

If we reflect on this transcript together, what do you notice about it that's different? Are you starting to see the negative beliefs that Kim had built up around her early experience with sex and pregnancy? It seemed to me that for Kim, her account was laden with guilt and shame. Kim firstly refers to her relationship being kept a secret from her parents. When we explored this further, I learned that her boyfriend was actually close friends with her father. She held on to the guilt around that for a long time.

Then there was her anxiety about getting the morning-after pill. It seems to Kim as though the doctor mirrored her feelings about herself in that instance – her feelings of shame around cheating and how the cheating had happened: drunk in a park. Kim is then 'caught in the act' as her boyfriend coincidentally walks into the doctor's surgery. When we discussed this, she remembered the feeling of her stomach dropping quite physically. It is as though her body had held onto that memory. My feeling is that her brain did too. Do you see how, if we think about it, Kim associated pregnancy with guilt, shame and avoidance?

Kim and I worked together to resolve this. She was able to forgive her teenage self. It was as though once we had talked about it, she was able to 'let go' of those negative feelings and instead reframe that time in her life with experience, compassion and kindness. By working together to make her implicit thoughts and feelings explicit, we unpicked her unconscious thoughts and beliefs and formed a new and authentic mindset – a pro-natal one. This is why I want to guide you through this same process.

All of the following exercises could, and arguably should, be done with your partner. Remember, it's not all on your shoulders. If it's just you, though, that's fine too. If there's someone close to you who you trust, you can work through it with them. Either way, I'm going to be here to guide you to get the most out of these exercises.

Exercise 1: The past: Visualisation

Visualisation is the first step to unlocking your past, as it's where your core beliefs about having a baby may have become set in your brain. Beliefs get rooted in a certain pathway like this – something of a neural rut, if you like. It could be that right now your brain is responding to several years of conditioning. Your brain may be honouring messages it has received in the past. If your brain could speak it might say, "Yes, I remember you telling me again and again and AGAIN that you don't want to be pregnant – I get it!" We need to reconfigure this.

If you visualise a point in time, what does it achieve? Well, visualising it means we can go back into it. We can revisit it. We can undo that thinking. We need to go back and amend it so that we can move forwards. We're basically using a time machine to see where something happened in your psychological network of connections. We will identify any outdated beliefs and, by revisiting the source of those beliefs, we can begin to resolve and revise them. We are going to learn about what happened and we're going to process them together.

So I am curious to know at this stage – what experiences or beliefs come to mind when you think about your relationship with having a baby? As I mentioned before, this first exercise is best done with someone else. Whoever you choose to work through this with you, the person will need to be open, curious and non-judgemental. This must be someone you can trust and can completely open up to. You must be prepared to share your deepest personal experiences.

Now, this may sound strange, but this does not automatically need to be your partner. Sometimes your partner is not the right person. If it is, then great, but if not, that's all right too. If you choose to do this exercise alone, then I would suggest you write it out for yourself in the style of a personal essay or journal.

Don't worry about the grammar, spelling or even presentation. Much more important here is to allow for a stream of your consciousness. In my experience your unconscious takes note when it sees the shift from implicit to explicit. This is why journaling is recognised as such an effective method of improving psychological well-being.

My tips for you:

- When you explain or write your stories and situations (there may well be more than one), slow everything down. I want you to tune into yourself.
- Pay particular attention to your body. Your body may well remember this time too, as we saw in the example previously when Kim's stomach dropped. Does your chest feel tight? Do you feel any butterflies in your tummy? Listen to your body.
- Make a note of any anxiety you feel as you recall things. Common emotions are fear, guilt, shame and anger. Tune in to these, they may be holding valuable information about what remains unresolved.

My tips for your listener:

- Be curious! You're going to become an emotional detective.
- Notice when the other person may start talking quickly or if something in their body or voice changes. Do they seem more anxious? More emotional? Ask them what they are feeling and remind them to slow down and be mindful.
- Be kind. Remember that this will be emotional; this will test them. Try not to judge them by how you are feeling, and be aware of downplaying the importance of their experiences. The experiences you hear may not be about you; they may well be about an ex. Or they may be about an experience that your partner has had around sex that you've never discussed before.
- Put yourself in the position of talking to your partner the way you would a friend. If someone's going to open up to you, you

have to be receptive. You have to mirror their experience.

- Don't go with your own reaction; go with the reaction the other person needs. Put their needs first. This will be difficult for them, but resist the temptation to rush to fix this.
- Check in with each other as you go through this. Make sure you're both okay to continue. If this simply brings up too much and you feel you can't do this, you need to consider using the services of an in-person therapist.

I have laid out three different visualisation techniques for you to try. I would suggest you give them all a go. Each of them attempts to achieve the same result (revisiting points in your past) but they go about it in slightly different ways. There is no 'one size fits all', so please feel free to mix them up and experiment.

You might have a good idea of when your beliefs around pregnancy formed, or you might not. Let's consider how we handle it when it's not obvious how, when or even why you started to have a negative belief around pregnancy. This could easily have been something innocuous someone close to you once said. They planted a thought in your brain which, over time, was repeated and became a deeply held belief.

If you are fortunate enough to know very well when the event (or events) took place in your past, then our job is a little easier. We want to change how you recall that event now. At the time you may have found it profoundly upsetting. You may have felt helpless, nervous or vulnerable. We will change it by going back to the event (or events) and reframing it from a place of understanding and compassion.

First technique: The time machine

Now you need to either write down what comes to mind or to describe the narrative out loud to someone else in as much detail as you can. Think about it carefully. This is just how we start, and we will take things slowly from here.

Take a deep breath and cast your mind back. Think back to when you started having sex or started learning about sex.

- What sorts of messages did you receive around pregnancy and having a baby?

- How did you learn about sex and pregnancy?
- Did you have a pregnancy scare?
- Did you have an unwanted pregnancy?
- Perhaps there were people or friends around you who were pregnant?
- What messages did you get from your parents, from school, from your peers even?
- How did you feel about your body?

In some cases there may have been trauma or abuse. In these cases it is imperative that you feel safe going into this visualisation. There is something about trauma that, when relived, can often make it feel as though it is happening in the present, and can cause great anxiety. If this exercise feels like it could be too much, it may be best approached by a Conceiving Conception Therapist. A list of approved therapists can be found at www.conceivingconception.com

When you feel ready, I'm going to ask you to go back to a scene you recalled that really resonates. Think about it like a scene in a film. For Kim, the scene that resonated the most took place in her doctor's surgery. As she experienced (or re-experienced) her stomach dropping, it seemed to be the part of the story that evoked the most emotional pain.

As I did with Kim, I'm going to ask you to go back to the first of the points in time you have identified. I want you to start thinking about the messages you received. If any of these stand out for you, I want us to explore them a bit more deeply. Can you tell me about the scene? What were you wearing? Who was there? How were you feeling?

Once you have described the narrative and can locate the scene and hold it in your mind, I would like to ask you to take a snapshot of that picture. What do you see? I want you to try to capture it in a single frame, as though time stands still and the scene is paused. I want you to now imagine you are going to enter that scene as the present-day you. I want you to go in and amend this. Sounds a little abstract, doesn't it? But I want you to try.

This time machine exercise is one you need to go through for each of the scenes you identified. Try to reframe what happened 'then' with what you know 'now'. If you think about it rationally, you know what you need to say to your younger self. You were younger then – of course you didn't want to get pregnant. In Kim's case, she spoke to her younger self and congratulated her for being responsible and taking care of herself. What's good about the future that you didn't know then? What needs to be healed? Take this opportunity to talk to your younger self with the knowledge and experiences of your present-day self.

If you have a partner, invite them to do this time-travelling exercise too.

Second technique: The safe place

In this technique I want you to really connect with your younger self. To do this through visualisation, you must create a safe place in your mind's eye. This is a place in which you feel secure, empowered and at ease. This could be a garden, a beach or simply anywhere you have been in your life where you felt at peace. Once you can visualise yourself in that safe place, you can begin a conversation with your younger self at the first time matters of pregnancy came to light. This is how I suggest you do this:

- It's important to relax, so please close your eyes and breathe deeply.
- Now I'd like you to imagine you're walking down a flight of steps.
- When you get to the bottom of the steps, you arrive in your safe place. Here you feel safe, confident and reassured.
- Before we do anything more, I'd like you to take it all in. Have a moment to just absorb your surroundings. Are there any special sights, smells or sounds you are experiencing?
- Once you're settled in your safe place, look over and notice your younger self approaching slowly.
- Wave to your younger self and get them to come over and join you. Give them a hug. Make them feel welcome.
- When you're both relaxed, ask your younger self your first question. This may be something like "How did you feel about possibly having a baby?" It's a good idea to ask your question

in age-appropriate language, not in the way you'd speak to someone your current age. Speak in the language you would have used when you were that younger person.

- Be patient and wait for them to answer.
- Tell them how much you love them and be sure to give them a reassuring hug.
- Thank them for coming to see you and wish them goodbye.
- When they have gone from view, it's time to leave your safe place. Make your way back to the steps and climb back up.
- Take a deep breath and open your eyes.

How was that exercise? This approach is by far the easiest way to attempt to identify your previously held beliefs. Another way is through meditation but, unless you're already comfortable with the concept of meditation, this would not be the place to learn. If you are, however, please give this exercise a try.

Connecting to your younger self through meditation is a passive process: simply breathe deeply, relax, allow yourself to witness your thoughts, and ask your question. For example, you might like to ask, "Dear younger self, when was the first time I became aware of pregnancy?"

Allow yourself to witness the thoughts that rise and fall within your mind. Your younger self may or may not decide to reveal the answer to you. Remember to be patient, loving and accepting. If your younger self doesn't want to reveal the answer, embrace that. It's important that you and your younger self feel safe, secure and ready.

You might like to repeat your question every now and then if nothing of significance arises inside your mind. This process could take anywhere from a couple of minutes to an hour or more.

Third technique: Through the ages

This final technique is something of a hybrid of the earlier ones, but you may find this approach works for you. I want you to go back in time to when you were born.

I want you to spend a couple of minutes just breathing deeply. Now imagine we go back in a time machine to your birth. As we go through each year – one, two, three, four, five, six and onwards – stop when you think there may have been some sort of message given to you about pregnancy, babies, children or family.

Explore that age. What was going on?

Now carry on. You're seven, eight, nine, ten, eleven, etc. Repeat this step and review at each notable point. Find photos of yourself at that age if you can. Not only is it helpful to have and hold these pictures for this exercise, it's also helpful to have them dotted around your home to remind you of your younger self.

Let's continue tomorrow because there are a few things we need to consider as we think about the exercises you've just completed. You might have identified more than one incident or event, for example. That's good – it means that for each one of those that you have identified, written down or discussed, you've already made progress. The simple act of revisiting these points in time is all a part of processing them. It's how we discover your overriding feelings, travel back in time and do something about them.

If you found the visualisation exercise emotional, take heart from that. The fact that it was emotional is all part of the processing you need to do. If you feel like you can hold on to this feeling and live with it for the time being, we will think about this together later in this workbook. If, however, it's overwhelming, then I invite you to go to the chapter on emotions, where I have some helpful exercises you can go through. Then you can come back here. This workbook is meant to be used as you need it, not as a strict programme of sequential steps. You may never have spoken to anyone about any of these events. Let's take a break now. We'll compete the second exercise tomorrow.

Exercise 2: The present: Your pregnant self

So far, we've talked about how your beliefs in the past may be affecting your ability to achieve what you desire in the present. We have begun to go back into these memories and reprogramme them so that your brain is more in tune with your current mindset. Now we need to give your brain a job – it likes to be active! We're going to create a new pathway for it, and to do that we need to do some spring cleaning in the dark and dusty parts of your subconscious. We need to throw out decades of old thoughts and beliefs and create a new mindset. The new mindset we want says "Yes! pregnancy is positive. This is what you want." Your brain has the absolute power to give you what you want. You just have to know how to talk to it. So how do you do that? Just how do you 'talk' to your brain? Let me show you.

After I've asked you to do this, I want you to put the book down for five minutes. Ready?

I want you to imagine you are pregnant. Don't just think of yourself with a pregnant tummy and move on, I want you to REALLY – THINK – ABOUT – IT. Sit with that thought and let it marinate... You're pregnant!

Now close the book – mark this page – and set a timer for five minutes. And think about it! Promise you will? Okay.

Welcome back. I'd like you to think about and notice how that made you feel. What was your gut reaction? This is important, so please make a note.

....

....

....

....

....

....

Now I am going to ask you to try to write a letter to the baby in you, where you, the writer, are pregnant. I want you to talk about your pregnancy. I want you to notice how your body is changing, how your body is growing, what it feels like to have a baby in your womb. Talk to your unborn baby. What do you want to say?

To help you, I've provided an example letter. In this example, the writer is talking to her baby. Some of you may have had miscarriages and you may find this exercise difficult. But we need to let your brain know that pregnancy is something you still desire. Take a look at what this could look like:

We are one. Our hearts beating together in your perfect cocoon. My tummy is hard, round and warm, perfectly protecting you while you float in splendid isolation. Sometimes you give me a knee, or a foot, or a hand against my sides to remind me you're there – I know you're there, my precious little one – Mummy's little fighter, I laugh.

We listen to music together as I go about my day. We talk for hours and set the world to rights. I tell you all of the things that have happened so you're up to speed when we meet. I stroke you through my tummy as we dance and sing and talk. Sometimes I imagine your hand touches mine on the other side. I smile when I think about this. We'll be holding hands soon, my love. While you grow inside me, so too does my love in my heart. I feel my heart could burst – how can it hold that much love?

Already I think about everything I do, eat and drink and how it affects us. Of course, I'm not drinking, but you have told me I really think bananas on pizza is a great idea. Only the best bananas for you, my little one. I want you to have the best I can give. My body is working its magic and growing, nourishing and strengthening you, ready for our first day together on the outside.

You've developed a love of music. I know you hear and feel it in there. I know how it settles you when I sing to you. You're lucky you can't hear me that clearly! I know you'll have your own taste in music when you're free, but for now you put up with mine. It's not all roses, rainbows, unicorns and moonbeams, though. Sometimes I ache and would pay any ransom for a back and foot rub. I've started snoring, a new trait I'm not sure your dad likes but it's good prep for sleepless nights to come. Sometimes I may be too tired to move and I may get a bit snappy with dad but it's part of the journey toward the most amazing place – the day you arrive with us, my sweet one.

Yesterday we had a bath and you did a very passable front crawl – or at least, that's what it felt like! I think we both had a good laugh about it – your elbows are pretty sharp! So is your sense of humour. I'm sure I feel you laughing at the most inappropriate moments – like when I had a jacuzzi moment in the tub!

If our life together so far is anything to go by, we're going to have the best time together when you're with us, my love. Till then…

So now you have a feel for what your letter could look like, please have a go. I would urge you to approach the letter from a place of hope. Remember – this is what you want, so your brain needs to be bought up to speed! However, it would be remiss to assume that this is possible for all. This book is designed to be a companion workbook, so if you aren't ready to complete this task yet then that's okay. But it is going to provide us with valuable information.

. . . .

. . . .

. . . .

. . . .

. . . .

. . . .

. . . .

How did you get on? Now I want you to reread your letter. If this letter feels like it is full of negative emotion, please take a look at chapter 8 which considers emotions, where I've provided a number of practical tips and exercises to help you process these feelings.

If this letter feels unwritable then don't worry. Move on to the following chapters and I'll leave it with you to circle back to it when you feel ready.

There won't be one single response to this exercise. So remember: be kind. Don't judge yourself. If you're not ready to write a letter like that, that's fine. If you can't do it, if you feel blocked, that's fine. If it brings up emotions you weren't expecting, that's fine too. Just be kind to them. Pay attention to how you're feeling and be kind.

If you've been able to complete this task, please read through your letter aloud with someone else if you can, even if that's down the phone. Reading this aloud with someone else is so very important. But be prepared; in my experience, this brings up a lot of emotion. This is understandable – it's what you desire, after all. Afterwards, I want you to remember this letter daily, so perhaps put a copy by your bedside or a copy on your phone. Remember: your job is reprogramming! Our brains respond to repetition, so read this letter daily either to yourself or to another person in order to send the message to your brain that pregnancy is good.

Consolidation

These exercises and techniques may well have left you feeling a little bit raw. So take your time with this. They are not meant to be rushed. It was brave of you to even attempt this. I don't underestimate the strength it's taken you to do this. You should also not finish these exercises thinking "I've not moved forward". All we're doing at this stage is going to the core, seeing what's there, noticing it and then starting to put in some techniques to reconfigure it.

I want to reinforce my earlier message that the mere act of working through these exercises and techniques is helping you move forward. I know you're not oversimplifying this and thinking that you've done enough to get pregnant. We both know that you cannot 'wish' yourself into pregnancy. All I'm doing is taking you through a method, and the first part of this method was to look at the origin. We will then solidify it and update it to align with your present desires around pregnancy.

It's only by going back that we are able to give you a fresh perspective on your past, and this new perspective will start to give you some control of your old belief. When you have control, you have the power to get rid of that outdated belief. In its place we're going to plant a new, pro-pregnancy one. Then we're going to help it grow.

The overriding message I hope you're getting is that this is all about healing these prior experiences, framing them with what you know now and sharing that knowledge and life experience with your younger self. In a therapeutic setting, what we've done in this chapter would be considered a first phase. It's a good foundation to build on. In a one-to-one setting, this could take a long time over multiple sessions, so don't rush it and don't forget about the exercises. Your regular rereading of your letter is so important. We're going to move through lots of different stages during this process, but they say every journey begins with a first step. This is your first step. Let's keep moving forward together.

Chapter 4

Your Body: Tuning in and Listening

Let me kick this chapter off by asking you a question. How are you and your womb getting along? It might seem like an abstract question but it's an important one, because it may well hold some previously hidden thoughts and feelings that we need to explore.

As joint fertility therapists (that's right – you are the therapist just as much as I am), you and I need to talk about all the activities you've been doing to help you get pregnant: period tracking, taking your temperature, monitoring your ovulation and your hormones. But we're going to talk about them on a different level to the one you've been used to. I want to talk about how these processes make you *feel*.

In this chapter we're also going to work on creating a relationship between your mind and your body. You may be asking yourself why we need to do this. What's the point? Well, the mind–body connection is important because if you have been trying to conceive for some time, have suffered miscarriage or are going through IVF treatment unsuccessfully, it's common to develop a feeling that your body has somewhat 'betrayed' you. In some way, even at a very deep level, you feel like your body has let you down.

Many women who have been through multiple rounds of IVF tell me that their body almost feels like it doesn't belong to them any longer. This way of thinking may well resonate with you wherever you are in your fertility journey. With many of my patients, I find that anxiety, trauma and unresolved events are living within the body. What could you be carrying in your body? What did you identify in the last chapter?

By working through these exercises, we may well uncover something that has remained hidden since before conceiving was even on the cards – something that we need to work through together. Very often with my patients it's these hidden feelings, thoughts and emotions that are standing in the way of fertility success. This is why it's so important that we work on re-establishing and reinforcing your own mind–body connection in order to create the authentic mindset we have been talking about.

Working on your mind–body connection sounds odd at first to most people I work with. After all, one sits alongside the other – right? We both know you've probably spent a lot of time checking your temperature and monitoring ovulation, etc. Well, as I mentioned earlier, it's not uncommon for people to find that the process of trying (and struggling) to become a parent can create something of a disconnect – a split between your mind and your physical body.

If we consider my earlier assertion that not only can infertility cause a disruption to your mindset but that your unreconciled mindset may be contributing to your infertility, then we need to apply the same thinking here. In this case, not only has infertility disrupted the relationship you have with your body – feelings of failure or betrayal – but perhaps now what's unresolved in your body could be a contributing factor to your infertility.

The exercises we will work through together in this chapter are intended to help you reconnect the dots, to rewire the connection between your body and your mind and, perhaps, to repair some of the damage that may have built up on your journey to date. There are several things for you to try in this chapter. I'd encourage you to take your time and work through them with a buddy. If you're unable to do that, please write down your thoughts and answers to the exercises. Speaking about the topics or writing them down helps significantly in making your unconscious conscious and, by extension, creating an authentic mindset.

It's often helpful to frame these exercises with how they have helped others before you. By working through these exercises together my hope is that, if there are any unconscious 'blocks' that may be lingering in the back of your mind, we will begin to tease these out to the surface. Once any blocks have surfaced, we will work through them together with further techniques which I have refined over many years. If you fully commit to these exercises and work through them in a thoughtful way, I believe that you will have a much healthier relationship with your womb.

Your body

How do you feel about your body? When we talk about your body, what does that bring up for you? Are you friends with your body? Through the process of trying to have a baby, a woman's body can quickly be viewed simply as a baby-making machine. When this 'machine' doesn't work as it should, this can get very stressful very quickly.

But your body is more than that. It's your flesh, your soul, your emotions. We cannot focus on just one element of our body – we must consider the whole. If there is a split between your mind and your body, or if you're constantly stressed but ignore your physical symptoms, you're likely causing a major disruption to your ability to have a healthy pro-natal mindset. Your body is central to this mindset.

So just how do we go about making sure that your psychoneuro-immunology is in balance?

We can start creating mind–body balance by tuning in to your body. The best way to do this is to conduct a mindfulness exercise. You may have done something like this before, especially if you've ever tried meditation. In this chapter we're going to do a simple 'body scan' exercise. By working on your mindfulness, we can increase your ability to recognise and then minimise any stress in your body. Mindfulness helps you to 'respond' rather than 'react' to stress. By increasing your mindful awareness, you'll be able to calmly manage the inevitable psychological, physiological and emotional ups and downs that accompany a period of infertility.

Exercise 1: The body scan

Body scanning works to break the cycle of physical and psychological tension caused by stress. Research shows that body scan meditation reduces stress, which in turn has physical benefits, including reduced inflammation. Inflammation feeds stress, and stress in turn affects our immune system. Stress in our immune system can lead to autoimmune disorders, one of which is unexplained infertility, which leads to more stress. We need to break this vicious cycle, and meditative body scans are a critical tool in doing just that.

I'd like you to read through the exercise and then find somewhere comfortable and quiet where you can relax. This could be an armchair or a couch, but I'd suggest you don't use your bed, because experience shows me that you'll probably fall sound asleep before you finish.

Sitting comfortably, I'd like you to take a deep breath in through your nose and out through your mouth. Take a few deep breaths like this and then gently close your eyes. I'd like you to focus on how your body feels right now. We're going to start at the top of your head and then we're going to gently scan down through your body, noticing what feels comfortable and what feels uncomfortable. I want you to pause and reflect on how each and every element feels. Please don't rush. Just pay attention to how your body feels as you slowly scan down all the way down to your toes. As you scan each part of your body ask yourself: how does that feel? Do you notice any pressure? Do you get a sense that there is any tension you're holding? We want to embody your experiences.

When you've completed your scan, I'd like you to make a note here of any areas which stood out for you. They may have felt tight. They may have been tingling. Anything at all that felt anything less than completely at ease, please note it down.

....

....

....

....

....

My sensations

Where?	What did I feel?

By mentally scanning yourself, you bring awareness to every single part of your body, noticing any aches, pains, tension or general discomfort. The goal is to get you to tune in and recognise stress so that you can better manage it. As is the aim of this whole book, it's about getting to know what is hurting you and how, by paying attention to it, we can start to heal it.

Sometimes we can get so caught up in stress and everyday life that we don't even realise the physical discomfort that is in our bodies – things like headaches, back or shoulder pain and muscle tension. These symptoms are highly likely to be connected to your emotional state of mind.

So let's say you've identified tension in your neck and shoulders. I want you to ask yourself: "What would I recommend to a friend to do about this?" Or even ask yourself: "What are my neck and shoulders trying to tell me? Do they need sleep? A massage?" The answer often lies in simply paying attention.

I find with my patients that the best results are achieved if we can find a way to perform this exercise daily, or even several times a day, so that it becomes less of a chore and more a part of your routine.

Danielle: *I've been doing the body scan thing we talked about.*
Louise: *Oh yeah? How did you get along?*
Danielle: *Well, I realised something. I realised that my hip hurts a lot more than I realised.*
Louise: *Your hip does?*
Danielle: *Yeah, it's an old injury. But I didn't realise, or, like, I didn't pay attention to how sore it was – day to day!*
Louise: *And it's really sore, hey?*
Danielle: *Yeah – it's really sore and I hadn't really noticed – I think that I've just become used to the pain.*
Louise: *I think it's really hard to be in pain all the time. It sounds like something we need to pay attention to.*

What Danielle and I learned together was that she had a tendency to ignore her pain. This meant that her body was holding unnecessary and counterproductive stress. This increased awareness prompted her to seek therapeutic treatment for her old injury, which meant she didn't have to be in pain any more. The upside of this was a significant reduction in stress.

Exercise 2: The mirror
This is a simple exercise but it can reveal a lot, mentally as well as physically.

We tend to think of looking in the mirror as a sign of narcissism or, on the flip side, something that can bring on feelings of inadequacy. But learning how to see yourself in your own reflection can increase your sense of self-awareness. In this exercise we want to use the mirror to increase your self-compassion. Infertility can be something of an emotional roller coaster and it's all too easy to be hard on yourself, so self-compassion is something we need to nurture. We're going to do this by working towards a more embodied sense of self – with all our perceived faults and imperfections.

So now I'd like you to try something. I'd like you to get yourself completely naked and then stand in front of a mirror (ideally something full-length – and definitely not while at work!) in all your glory – as nature intended. For some people this is liberating, while for others it's not a pleasant experience. I wonder where you sit on that spectrum. Let's find out, shall we?

Once you're naked in front of your mirror, I'd like you to set a timer for three (long) minutes.

Much as we did in the previous exercise, I want you to take some deep breaths and then, slowly, scan yourself from your head to your toes. Don't rush – you've got three minutes, after all. As you scan your body I want you to take in all the details and pay attention to how you feel about each part. Notice the tone of your internal monologue as you complete this scan. I'll wager that right now the way you are thinking and feeling about yourself is much harsher than the way you would think and feel about others.

When you're done, pop some clothes back on (we don't want to scare the neighbours) and make some notes in the following space. Use the notes pages in the back of the workbook if you need more space. Don't simply list your body parts like a medical student – I want to really know what you love about your body and what you don't love as much. So for each body part I want you to add a few words that show your feelings about that particular part of you.

What I love and how that makes me feel	How do I feel about the parts I think are less desirable?

Mirrors can evoke strong feelings in all of us. Our desire to be seen and reflected is basic and innate. As children, we learn to understand ourselves through the reflections of those around us. In fact, psychologists have found that face-to-face contact is essential for our social and emotional development. It's these strong feelings that make mirrors such incredibly powerful tools for changing our perspective. It's only by focusing on the parts of ourselves that are usually hidden from the world that we can begin to focus on the parts we feel are less than desirable. These are the parts we need to consider. We need to understand how your perception of your body could potentially be holding back your pro-fertility mindset. As we're not usually surrounded by mirrors, it could be argued that we lose touch with our own face-to-face contact. This is our opportunity to reconnect.

Let's take a moment now to stop and consider anything you listed in the right-hand column. If you haven't listed anything, I'd encourage you to repeat the exercise – no one is perfect. Our job is to tease out any unconscious blocks that may be presented as something that you don't like about your body, because anything you've put in that right-hand column indicates something we need to work on further – we need to get to the bottom of those feelings (or, indeed, your feelings about your bottom!).

If there is something you really don't like about your body, why is that? Was there a time when you liked your body? What has changed since then?

One patient I asked to do this exercise broke down in tears when she realised how much pain her physical body was harbouring:

> **Nina:** *I hated that mirror exercise. I only did it this morning as I knew we would have to talk about it!*
>
> **Louise:** *Well, thank you for doing it. I know it's not easy, but I am curious: what do you think felt so difficult for you, because it sounds like you may have been putting it off?*
>
> **Nina:** *'Cause…I don't look at my body! I don't want to look at it. I don't even want my partner looking at it.*
>
> **Louise:** *Gosh – can you tell me more?*
>
> **Nina:** *It's gross. It feels gross. Everyone can see how gross I am.*
>
> **Louise:** *Gross? Gross is a pretty harsh way of talking about yourself.*
>
> **Nina:** *Yeah, it is. But it's ugly! It's scarred, it's bloated – it looks old! Tired!*
>
> **Louise:** *I wonder what your body has been through for it to feel this way to you, Nina?*
>
> **Nina:** *(crying) Just…just…well, the IVF, the miscarriage, the whole experience in hospital, being on the same ward as women delivering, the adhesions.*

Louise: *Your body has been through too much, hey?*
Nina: *(crying)* Yes.
Louise: *It's too much. Your poor body.*

As you can see, it was as though Nina was reading her own sense of self through the perceptions she felt other people had of her. She had come to be completely reliant on how she believed others viewed her because she refused to look at herself. This mirror exercise began to uncover her belief – to bring it from her unconscious so that we could address it consciously. The more she looked at herself, the more she was able to look empathetically at her body and the things it had been through. By doing this she was empowered to reconnect with herself. When we talked through her internal negative commentary, we began to find parts of herself she felt at ease with, that she felt proud of. We began the process of healing the psychological and physical pain that her infertility had caused. Rather than disconnecting from it, even though it was painful, she was able to re-establish a healthy mind–body connection.

What are some of the thoughts that went through your mind when you stood in front of the mirror? Commonly they're negative and critical. If they're not – great! But we know how hard we can be on ourselves. I want you to tune in to how these thoughts made you feel. Anxious, sad? Angry, frustrated, guilty? Embarrassed?

Learning to tune into yourself and your image as it really is will not turn you into a narcissist. The outcome is usually quite the opposite. Our aim here is that you learn new ways of being present with yourself. By being more present with yourself, you are more able to manage the intensity of your emotions. This exercise will help you to tap into a new awareness – an awareness that is framed in the light of positivity.

Exercise 3: Conversations with your womb

In this next exercise I hope to uncover any unease you may feel about your body – specifically your womb. If you have experienced emotional stress or trauma, your womb might be holding onto tension. As with this whole workbook, our aim here is to clear any emotional blockages you may be unconsciously harbouring. I want to help you to prepare to welcome your baby into your womb and into your life.

If I asked you how you feel about your womb, what would you say? It's important here that you start thinking about your womb as part of your whole body – the whole you – not just as a baby-making organ. In other words, I want you to start thinking of it as something more than the sum of its parts and not as something purely functional.

> **Louise:** *Can I ask, if you picture your womb in your mind's eye, what comes up for you?*
> **Fran:** *Um, I can't really picture it. I just see, like, a textbook version.*
> **Louise:** *So what does that look like?*
> **Fran:** *Well, you know…pink with fluffy bits.*
> **Louise:** *Okay – that's the textbook one – how about yours? Take your time. Think about your body, your womb. What do you see?*
> **Fran:** *I don't know why, and I can't really explain this, but I want to say it's green and thick with tar.*
> **Louise:** *Green and thick with tar. Okay, interesting. Let's not judge it, let's just think about it some more.*

Sometimes just asking the question gives us much information. Without a doubt there was something that Fran felt was toxic about her womb. We explored this together and it actually linked back to a sexual memory for Fran. It needed our attention. It needed some healing so that it no longer felt toxic for her.

You see, your womb is something very special. As babies, we started learning in the womb. We listened to music; we learned the sounds of our mother's voice. We don't remember it, but we had experiences even then.

This is going to sound silly for me to ask, but how was your gestation? What was it like in the womb when you were forming in there? While you're unlikely to have such early memories, how you feel about the womb will shine a light on your deeper feelings about it. Womb visualisation is just one way we can start to think about things differently.

So, over to you. What does your womb look like? Please make some notes here.

My womb is…

....

....

....

....

....

....

....

....

....

....

....

....

Let's review what you wrote down. What does it make you think? What does your inner fertility therapist make of this? Is there anything that might make them sit up and take note? What might need some special attention? Do any blockages come to mind?

Many women have what I call 'energetic blockages' within their womb. By this I mean that a connection has been blocked, tarnished, maybe even hurt. This leaves us disconnected from the ideal vision of our own womb. To re-establish this connection we need to clear, heal and rebalance how you feel about your womb. That starts by listening to your own womb and hearing what she has to say.

If your womb could speak right now, what would she say? The first thought that comes to mind is usually "Make me pregnant!" But let's go deeper. What else might she say? What does she need you to hear?

....

....

....

....

....

....

....

....

....

....

Exercise 4: Connecting with your womb

This exercise is a starting point and, based on what you might discover during this special womb journey, you might want to consider consulting your creativity, your significant other, your friend and/or perhaps a therapist on this journey. But let's try to do this between us for now. What would your inner fertility therapist notice and how do they think they can facilitate healing? Let's try this exercise as something of a meditation.

I want you to find somewhere quiet and peaceful where you can sit for a few minutes uninterrupted.

Now breathe, slowly and steadily. Bring your consciousness to your breath. You know the drill: in through the nose, out through the mouth. Nice and deep.

Now, try bringing an awareness to your womb centre and just allow yourself to listen, to feel, sense and experience your womb. Notice: is it warm or cool, dark or light? There may be blockages; there may not be. There may be feelings that you haven't felt in a long time or even that you have never felt before. It's okay. This is very personal and may feel quite intense. Just listen and allow yourself to experience your womb.

Breathe, listen and hear the silent echoes of what you and your womb have been through together. Let your womb know that you are listening to whatever she needs to share without judgement, without blame, without shame.

Now take a deep breath, release and return to your normal breathing pattern.

When you have completed this exercise take a few moments to reflect, write your thoughts in this workbook and talk to others.

....

....

....

....

....

....

....

As we have considered your relationship with your womb, there is plenty of value in performing the same exercise with your vagina. After all, she has a pretty important role to play too. It may not be a bad idea to ask her a similar line of questioning. And let's not leave the boys out of the conversation. When it comes to penises, testicles and sperm, this type of exercise is just as valuable in exploring and discovering your more deeply held feelings.

Exercise 5: Period tracking

Notwithstanding the softer aspects of my therapeutic approach, there are some hard and fast things you also need to do in order to maximise your chances of success. Let's consider your periods and whether you're really giving them the attention they need.

For this exercise, I'd like you to fill in the following tracker every day. I want you to simply fill in the relevant circles and, if possible, also take your temperature. Try to do this around the same time every day (if you're not already doing something similar) so you can make it a routine, but don't beat yourself up if you don't manage to do it at the same time or if you miss a day. I have found early evening is a good time to do this, as it's an opportunity to look back on how you found your day and what your energy and mood were like. If you're one of the lucky ones who feels amazing first thing in the morning, then that works too. As I said, consistent timing is helpful here. We're trying to create an increased awareness of your body. Of course, you've most likely done some of this already in your fertility journey, but in this exercise we are adding another dimension and considering your emotions too.

If you're not experiencing a period, just leave the Flow column blank. For the Energy column, I want you to rate your energy level today on a scale of Low, Medium or High. The same goes for your general mood in the 'Mood' column and, if you're able to, please record your temperature. Finally, please take a little time to consider how you're feeling and make a note of it.

Before you start scribbling, please feel free to photocopy this table so you can complete more than one month of data, as this will give you a more complete picture.

Day	Flow (L-M-H)			Energy (L-M-H)			Mood (L-M-H)			Temp	How do you feel?
1	O	O	O	O	O	O	O	O	O		
2	O	O	O	O	O	O	O	O	O		
3	O	O	O	O	O	O	O	O	O		
4	O	O	O	O	O	O	O	O	O		
5	O	O	O	O	O	O	O	O	O		
6	O	O	O	O	O	O	O	O	O		
7	O	O	O	O	O	O	O	O	O		
8	O	O	O	O	O	O	O	O	O		
9	O	O	O	O	O	O	O	O	O		
10	O	O	O	O	O	O	O	O	O		
11	O	O	O	O	O	O	O	O	O		
12	O	O	O	O	O	O	O	O	O		
13	O	O	O	O	O	O	O	O	O		
14	O	O	O	O	O	O	O	O	O		
15	O	O	O	O	O	O	O	O	O		
16	O	O	O	O	O	O	O	O	O		
17	O	O	O	O	O	O	O	O	O		
18	O	O	O	O	O	O	O	O	O		
19	O	O	O	O	O	O	O	O	O		
20	O	O	O	O	O	O	O	O	O		
21	O	O	O	O	O	O	O	O	O		
22	O	O	O	O	O	O	O	O	O		
23	O	O	O	O	O	O	O	O	O		
24	O	O	O	O	O	O	O	O	O		
25	O	O	O	O	O	O	O	O	O		
26	O	O	O	O	O	O	O	O	O		
27	O	O	O	O	O	O	O	O	O		
28	O	O	O	O	O	O	O	O	O		
29	O	O	O	O	O	O	O	O	O		
30	O	O	O	O	O	O	O	O	O		
31	O	O	O	O	O	O	O	O	O		

By completing this simple exercise on a daily basis, we are achieving something very important. We are strengthening your mind–body connection. The beauty of this exercise is that you can begin to recognise what's happening in your body and how it's impacting your mind.

Without question, stress affects you. Critically, it also affects your fertility, as we talked about in Chapter 1. Stress can raise your body temperature because your systems are working harder, which is why we need to track the changes in your body. If, through close monitoring and tracking, we are able to tune in to when you're going to be more stressed, we can start to prepare you to be a little more understanding, compassionate and kind to yourself.

The simple act of paying attention to your body is what we're focused on. This exercise brings an increased awareness of your body through your mind. Your body responds to the way that you think. And how you think can (and does) affect how you feel. In the past, fertility interventions have focused purely on the physical aspects of you. Similarly, I don't want to fall into the trap of focusing exclusively on your mind. My job is to connect the dots and bring it all together – to bring you all together. Your mind–body connection is critical to overcoming anything which may be blocking your pregnancy journey.

Hormone fluctuations and ovulation

It's helpful to highlight just what's going on with your body when you're trying to conceive. The two hormones that play a critical role in the process are known as LH and E3G.

LH stands for 'luteinizing hormone', and it's produced by your pituitary gland (more on the importance of this later). Your body constantly generates a low level of LH, but just before you ovulate, your body makes much more. This is known as the 'LH surge'. Typically, this surge begins 24–36 hours before you ovulate.

Your E3G hormones are produced when oestrogen breaks down in your body. It causes the surface in your cervix to become extra-slippery. This slippery surface helps sperm to swim more easily, which in turn increases your chances of getting pregnant.

As you can see from the chart below, these two important hormones are always present but they spike once a month – just when you ovulate.

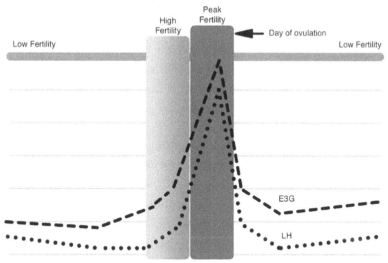

Your LH surge (the dotted line here) is interesting because it represents when you will be at your most fertile and pumping out sexual hormones which make you sexually attractive. This is something of an evolutionary trick to get your 'mate' to – well, *mate*. Your body knows when you're ovulating and so triggers it to be the most sexually attractive it can be. You may feel tired from work and fed up with all the sex but you can't fight evolution – your LH surge is responsible for this. These hormone waves are critical to your ability to conceive. They mess about with your emotions but, in the words of stress reduction master Jon Kabat-Zinn, "You can't stop the waves but you can learn to surf."

Learning to surf is why I want you to complete this daily checklist. We're trying to illustrate the patterns of your cycle on this checklist in order to make life a little easier for you. Instead of fighting against the tides of your cycle, go with it. You're going to feel more irritable, so what can you do to make yourself feel better? I want to help you adopt a more self-caring approach.

Our job as fertility therapists is to attune you to your body in much the same way as I attune myself to my patients in a therapeutic setting. Let me give you an example of why this is so important.

I had a patient whom I saw weekly for several months. After a while

I began to recognise a pattern in her mood, and before long I knew exactly when she would feel more chaotic, because it tied in with her monthly cycle. I had noticed it but she had not. When I explained to her that it was not that she was unable to cope but that it was her hormone surge that was messing with her moods, she was able to ride the wave much better. By making her hormone changes part of her conscious thought, she felt less overwhelmed because she knew to take good care of herself that week and treat herself with compassion and kindness.

So now I'd like you to tune in to yourself so that you too can become acutely aware of your body and its changes. We all know how your mood changes in the month. Now we need to join the dots to understand exactly how your hormones affect your mood. And more than that, I want you to connect with the emotional part of the process.

Why is that important? As I said earlier, as part of the process of trying and failing to conceive or carry to term, your mind and body can become split. It's not uncommon for women to view ovulation as simply the time when they can get pregnant. When they don't fall pregnant, their next period serves to remind them that their most recent attempt at pregnancy failed. Every new period feels like another punch in the guts. I hear this all too often, and for women who have suffered a miscarriage, the emotional impact of getting a new period is doubly painful.

Because of where you are on your journey, you may have inadvertently created a mind–body split. By making you more aware and in tune with your body, we're trying to reconnect those two pieces of yourself. The days of letting things 'just happen' are gone. From now on we're going to sit up, pay attention and listen to your body.

It's only by going through these exercises and tuning in to your body that we will get closer to the optimal conditions for your successful pregnancy mindset. And remember that you're not only tuning into your body – you're tuning into your emotions as well. Your emotions are connected to your hormones, but the experience of this relationship is different for everyone. So it's important that you understand what's happening to *you*.

Becoming more consciously aware of how you feel is especially important when it comes to stress. This is because, to varying degrees, stress constantly activates our fight-flight-freeze response. And since most of the experiences that cause us stress are not immediate threats to our lives – as they would have been for our ancestors – the fight-flight-freeze stress response has become inappropriate for modern life.

Worse still, the stress response has been shown to make us unwell by causing unnecessary wear and tear on our bodies, much like a car that is constantly driven with its accelerator pushed to the floor. Inevitably, we break down.

We need to get your mindset and your body working in concert. We know we've hit the sweet spot when you start becoming your own therapist, when you understand how to nurture and cultivate your own awareness. A fundamental part of this is understanding what it's like to be in your body. What does it mean to you to have the body that you have? Let's give this some thought.

....

....

....

....

....

....

....

....

....

....

Infertility and womanhood

In 1949, the French philosopher Simone de Beauvoir asserted that "One is not born, but rather becomes, a woman." What she meant was that despite the simple fact that our bodies at birth are shown as male or female, it is the processes of society that transform each of us into the people we become.

In our society, a woman's childbearing ability can often be closely linked to her status as a woman. If a woman is infertile, she may feel unfeminine. If a man is infertile, he may feel emasculated.

Let's take a look at Luca when she was talking about a connection between her unexplained infertility and womanhood:

> **Luca:** *There is a stigma that I wish didn't exist – for a woman feeling less like a woman.*
> **Louise:** *That's interesting – what do you mean?*
> **Luca:** *Being barren! Doesn't make you feel very worthy, I suppose. Look at everyone just getting pregnant so easily… And here I am…barren! (laughs)*

Luca was, as is so common with women experiencing infertility, comparing herself to everyone else around her. She felt "less like a woman" and less "worthy" because she couldn't conceive. In other words, Luca viewed herself in society as something less than her fertile counterparts. Let's take a closer look at what may be going on for you and what being a woman means to you.

Exercise 6: What does your body mean to you?

Being a woman means many different things to different people, because we are all a reflection of our experiences to date. For some, being a woman may have been traumatic. For others, being a woman may have created a sexual environment that they were not old enough to be in. Others have found that being a woman created jealousy or competition. If we consider being a woman in the workplace today, while we've certainly come a long way, there is still a massive gap in gender equality.

So let me pose some questions for you that may elicit a feeling in your gut.

- Do you feel like you're treated equally?
- What makes it difficult to be in your body?
- What makes it easy to be in your body?
- What is it like to be in your body?
- Who is the person beyond the labels?
- What strengths, gifts, talents and perspectives do you bring to this moment?
- Do you feel safe in your body?

With these sorts of questions I'm trying to draw out, essentially, what it means to be you – the uniquely individual and lovely you.

I want to encourage you to consider all the questions above, but I also want you to make a note of those that are particularly important to you. I'd also like you to discuss your answers to these questions with your buddy (or at least write them down). Try to explore this subject of gender assignment as much as you can. My desire, after all is said and done, is that we look at ourselves with a sense of curiosity and seek to know – really know – ourselves.

Consolidation

The exercises in this chapter all attempt to bring your mind and body back into a healthy relationship. Your body isn't just a vessel – it is connected to your thoughts, feelings and experiences. You are, after all, more than just a baby-making machine. Through these exercises I wanted you to form a mindful relationship with your body, and specifically with your womb. I wanted you to tune in and see what you and your inner fertility therapist need to pay special attention to.

Every trauma, whether it occurs in a physiological, cognitive, emotional or interpersonal form, affects the physical body. The healing of trauma also begins in the body. Your body is the accurate history of your experiences in life; therefore it's essential that we include your body in the healing process. Similarly, we must bring mindfulness to the processes at work in your body.

So, let's say that in this equation, pregnancy is the goal. To reach this goal, you need to have an authentic mindset. We now understand that your relationship with your body is critical to that mindset. I'm not saying that you must be in love with your body, but you must be kind and compassionate to it. Now let's add to the equation that there may be something unconsciously blocking your pregnancy goal, and that any blocks may be due to unresolved conflicts that might be living in your body and have yet to be addressed. Addressing and healing these conflicts is critical to achieving your goal.

So let's bring it all together. What have you learned in this chapter? What stands out for you and what does your inner fertility therapist need to pay attention to? What would you say now to my opening question: how's your relationship with your womb? Write your thoughts below. As you continue through this workbook, keep up with the daily checklist so that you can become more and more in tune with both your body and your mind. Remember: we're reconnecting the two and integrating all parts of you. This is vital for your progress towards fertility.

....

....

....

....

....

....

....

....

....

....

Chapter 5

Getting to Know Yourself:
Becoming Your Own Therapist

You're working through this book because you're curious about what could be going on to prevent you from having a baby. Until now, you've been using typical fertility approaches to try to figure it out. My job is to show you how to think about things in a different way, to question in a different way, to assess your situation in a different way. In this workbook I talk about you becoming 'your own fertility therapist', but what does this actually mean?

My approach to therapy is the same with every patient I work with, no matter why they have come to see me: I first make a thorough assessment. It's only by doing this that I can work out how to help them most effectively. This assessment often involves asking questions that don't seem relevant to their fertility journey – questions that make them say "I'd never even thought about that!" Similarly, in this workbook I need us to consider many different aspects of psychology that will help me to help you. I'm going to ask you to consider questions which would, not unreasonably, never have occurred to you to ask yourself. The biggest question I ask in this area is: "Have you had any traumas you think I should know about?" Their gut reaction – perhaps like yours when you initially consider this question – is "No." But once they, and you, have had time to let that question really sink in and get past your instinctive answer, they often find themselves saying, "Well…apart from this one time when…" This is when I often hear about something that's caused a lot of psychological pain.

So what's going on? Why does everyone initially dismiss that question? I believe it has a lot to do with self-protection. This is understandable. If you consider this question in a one-to-one setting, we've only just met. Your perception of past events is one thing, but when you say it aloud, or perhaps write it down, it makes you think about it in a different way. It makes it real. The message here for you is: let's be open to exploring your past, your story.

The simple act of acknowledging your past and speaking your story out loud allows the processing part of your mind to do its job: to process. This is especially true in the context of creating a realistic and authentic mindset and, for many, it is why they come to therapy. Something may have happened in the past which hasn't yet been fully processed and which therefore has not been made conscious. And as we know, your past can negatively affect your present in ways you may not previously have considered.

Becoming your own inner therapist as part of the therapeutic process means that, by the end of therapy, you can work things out for yourself through awareness and by using the tools I have shared. I want you to trust that you can learn how to do what I do for yourself. This workbook is in many ways a manual for you to become your own fertility therapist. In this chapter I need you to become something of a constantly probing detective who simply doesn't accept the first answer.

Becoming your own inner therapist doesn't always mean working by yourself, however. Of course, if you work slowly and methodically there is plenty of benefit in working through this chapter on your own. But if there is an opportunity to work through these exercises with a buddy, you'll get even more out of it. If you find yourself reluctant to talk about these issues with someone else (this does not have to be your partner), it could be because these subjects are pointing to a potential block. This is a good early indication of something we might need to pay special attention to and process.

If you do decide to work through this chapter with a buddy,

different thoughts and questions will come out. It's a little like when you work or socialise with someone regularly – you tend to have certain predictable conversations with them and develop something of a conversational cadence. If your relationship with them changes – for example from platonic to romantic – the conversation, questions and answers will become very different. The dynamic shifts. It's that kind of shift in conversation that I want you to achieve by working through this chapter, which is why reflecting on your answers with someone else can be particularly helpful.

If you work through this on your own, you're not really changing the dynamic. Your narrative will be, let's say, predictable. Working with a buddy will help to draw you out of your comfort zone, because if your buddy asks you the questions instead of you asking them to yourself, you'll automatically approach them in a different way. This is your opportunity to think about these things with someone else, and therefore from a different point of view.

While working through with a buddy is the ideal situation, if this isn't possible then you can create the same kind of shift in dynamic by writing down your answers as you go. Your challenge is to *really* challenge yourself. The simple act of writing things down activates different neural pathways, and this movement of thoughts from your mind to paper is the same as moving thoughts from your mind to your therapist or buddy. The key here is not just to write down and move on, but to reflect on what you have written and to process it fully.

The act of writing down also makes you accountable for your words. It makes you take note and move that energy to another place – from your unconscious to your conscious. At a deeper level, this exercise is about investing your time. If you care enough to spend time writing it down, you care enough to think about it, to reflect on it. It's about being curious and mindful.

These days, who can honestly say that they take the time to just think about themselves? Most of us feel we're just too busy. It may be that we're taking care of other people but not taking care of ourselves. Very few of us feel that we can invest time in thinking about ourselves, so that's what we're going to make time to do in this chapter.

In movies we often hear people asking "So what's your story?" – because everyone has a past, a background, a reason for being as they are. In this chapter I want to help you to formulate that story – whether with a buddy or by writing it down. This will help you think about yourself in a way that you might not have done before. So let's take a look back over your life to date, with an emphasis on understanding your complete story – not just the fertility bits.

The process looks a little like this:

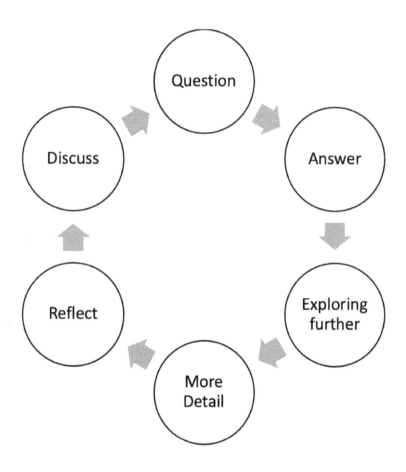

In a therapeutic assessment I start with a question, and when I hear the first answer I start to probe a little further. I resist the temptation to move quickly on to the next question, all the while paying close attention to any unconscious actions or reactions. These are indications of what I call your 'emotional thermometer'. In this way I get to the detail behind the patient's answer to the question, which enables us to reflect on what we have uncovered – "What do you think that means?"

The following questions are designed to draw out different memories, feelings and sensations. But my first question for you is this: how does the thought of this type of questioning make you feel? Notice your reaction. Do you feel excited? Nervous? What could these feelings potentially tell your inner fertility therapist?

So we have begun. That first question is designed to encourage you to become something of a detective. You need to approach this with a sense of curiosity, to build the same sort of understanding of yourself that I would as your therapist. How do I build up an understanding of you? By asking questions much like those you're about to work through. We need to work through these questions and study your responses, so I want you to review my comments following the questions and then go over them again. Crucially, I'm going to ask you to question your response. We need to notice your gut reaction to the questions and then explore it further.

Above I mentioned the emotional thermometer. By this I mean that I'm looking for sudden changes in emotional 'temperature' from my patients – for any flickers or a sense of unease that results from a particular line of questioning. I'd like you also to notice how you feel when you think about these questions. If one question in particular elicits a strong response – perhaps it makes you want to stop doing the exercise or makes you feel excited about this part of the process – then that is your thermometer shouting "THIS IS IMPORTANT! YOU NEED TO PAY ATTENTION TO THIS!"

In my experience with other patients, there is a high probability that working through these questions will trigger something in you. Be alert and ready to spot the signs, and remember that this is fact-finding – it's about spotting when you're saying one thing but your body is 'speaking' something completely different. It's all about connecting your mind with your body.

You're welcome to write your thoughts down here in the workbook. This is essential if you're working through these questions on your own, and optional if you're answering them with a buddy. Please also remember that what we're doing here is confidential and personal, so don't leave your workbook lying around.

....

....

....

....

....

....

....

....

....

....

Exercise 1: Outcome measures

You may be wondering why I am asking you about 'outcomes' at the start of these exercises. Well, it's because we need some sort of a baseline to check against at the end. I want to ease you into this work, and the best way to do that is with some short, quick questions. Some of these may seem similar to others, but that's just my way of getting you to think about the same topic from lots of different angles. One of those angles could connect to a completely different pathway and that could be critical, so just go with it.

I often use these outcome measures at the beginning and end of a block of sessions when I am working with someone, as they are a quick and easy way to measure progress.

This questionnaire is useful to establish a baseline for where you are and how you feel right now. I would suggest that you return to it and re-score yourself once you have completed all the chapters in this workbook.

Please mark yourself on a scale of 1 to 5, where 1 is 'I strongly disagree' and 5 is 'I strongly agree'.

I strongly disagree	I somewhat disagree	I feel neutral	I somewhat agree	I strongly agree
1	2	3	4	5

Statement	Score Today	Review Score (at a later date)
When it comes to important relationships, I know I can keep them going.		
My ability to deal with conflict remains strong despite the challenges I am facing.		
I enjoy seeing my friends and other social interactions.		
I feel at ease with everything going on in my life at the moment.		
Everything in my life is going the way I want it to.		
I prioritise my mental health.		
When I consider the future, I feel optimistic.		
I feel physically fit and well.		
I can find joy in life, events and things.		
I am kind to myself.		

So how do your results make you feel? It would be good to spend some time reflecting on these alone initially and then perhaps with your buddy.

Exercise 2: The assessment

This exercise is how I perform my initial assessment with a patient. I can't stress enough that you need to approach this exercise in a non-judgemental way with openness and kindness. These questions are about the core of you, and some of the answers may be painful. When I ask these questions in person, I make sure that I'm taking care of my patient as we work through them. I'm going to trust you to take care of yourself. If it all gets too much, please take a break and return to this later. Let's begin.

1.   What brings you to therapy?

....

....

2.   When I ask this question I say nothing else, but just listen to what they have to say. So how about you? What made you buy this workbook? Apart from the obvious, what made you buy it now? What's happened? I need you to consider what was the trigger to take the step to go through this workbook.

....

....

3.   What goes through your mind when you feel like this?

....

....

4. Explore this a little more, and remember: we're not settling for your first answer.

....

....

5. What physical symptoms do you notice?

....

....

6. Consider how these feelings make you feel physically.

....

....

7. How do you cope?

....

....

8. What helps?

....

....

....

9. What helps initially but eventually makes you feel worse?

....

....

10. What does this tell your inner fertility therapist?

....

....

11. How do you think therapy may help?

....

....

12. Now we understand why you're here, how do you think having your own inner fertility therapist might help you?

....

....

13. What do you find triggers your symptoms on a day-to-day basis?

....

....

14. This could be things such as social media. So what are your triggers?

....

....

....

15. When/where/with whom is the problem worse?

....

....

16. Let's add some context – what circumstances are particularly difficult?

....

....

17. What do you do to feel better?

....

....

18. The real question here is: does it actually end up making you feel better in the longer term?

....

....

19. What makes it feel worse?

....

....

20. What things are you doing more or less of because of how you are feeling?

....

....

21. Now I'd like to start to understand your fertility story. How long have you been trying to have a baby? When did you start?

....

....

This is a really important question because I want you to try to write this out chronologically. So when did you decide that you were going to try? Did you actively decide to try? I want you to talk about the genesis of the thought – about your 'conceiving' that conception. After that decision, then what happened? I want you to list it all. To get you thinking about it all, also consider these questions:

- How long have you tried naturally?

....

....

- Have you had rounds of IVF?

....

....

- Have you ever been pregnant?

....

....

- Have you experienced any miscarriages? You may or may not be aware that miscarriage is an important part of this story. It is, so take your time with this.

....

....

- Have you had a 'biochemical' pregnancy?

....

....

- Have you had an ectopic pregnancy?

....

....

- Are you currently undergoing treatment?

....

....

- Have you had treatment in the past?

....

....

- Do you already have any children?

....

....

    – If yes, how was the pregnancy? (in detail)

....

....

....

....

....

....

....

....

–   How was the birth? (again, I want detail)

....

....

....

....

–   How have your relationships been affected?

....

....

....

....

–   What impact has this problem had on your work/
    family/hobbies/social life?

....

....

Again, I need you to be a detective here. Together we are looking for signs of how you're really feeling. What is your thermometer saying?

Now that you have completed this exercise, I'll leave it to you to decide if you want to continue with the next one or if you want to take a break. Having a meaningful pause between these exercises allows you some time and space to consider your answers and, more importantly, any emotions which may have come up. Unlike a typical in-person therapy session, we have the luxury of being able to take a break. Having an opportunity to ruminate on what's just taken place is part of the therapeutic process, so please don't rush.

Exercise 3: Quick-fire questions

The following questions aim to identify any anxiety. While these questions may seem trivial – irrelevant, even – this is where we have the tantalising potential to get to the really good stuff!

What we're trying to do here is work out if you're holding any anxiety. These questions aim to bring that out. All I'm looking for here is your initial, gut-feeling, yes/no answer to these questions, so just write a quick Y or N next to each as you race through them.

Ready?... Set... Go!

1. Do you have any thoughts/images/impulses or rituals that you can't easily stop?
2. Do you try to ignore these or put them out of your mind?
3. Are you uncomfortable or embarrassed being at the centre of attention?
4. Do you avoid work/social situations where you feel you may be scrutinised?
5. Do you worry a lot of the time about a variety of topics?
6. Do you worry about worrying?
7. Are you afraid of going out of the house, being in crowds or taking public transport?
8. Are you overly concerned you might have a serious illness that doctors haven't found?

Anxiety is a tricky thing to identify, so the idea here is just to get you thinking about how you think. It's about tuning in and nurturing your inner therapist. So what stood out for you among these questions? Do we need to call on the detective to probe further? I want to help you reach the next stage of our investigations, which is finding out what any anxiety could be connected to. That's why I want you to write down as much as you can here, because this will help us when we consider anxiety later in the anxiety chapter.

Exercise 4: Important events

In this exercise I want us to take another look at any important or traumatic events. When I bring this up with my patients, they typically say "No, I've not experienced any trauma" – and then almost immediately go on to tell me about something traumatic in their past! Your trauma might not be dramatic or shocking – what we're looking for here is anything that has caused you to feel psychological pain.

Let's take a look at how one of these sessions went with Sophie:

Louise: *Okay, sometimes this is bit of a difficult question. But I would like you to tell me about any traumatic events that you think may be important for me to know about.*

Sophie: *No, not really, er, no.*

Louise: *Really?*

Sophie: *Well, my parents got divorced. But I was nine. It was fine.*

Louise: *It was fine?*

Sophie: *Well, we didn't really talk about what happened. They were fighting a lot. So they got divorced and my dad moved out.*

Louise: *What did you understand about it, I wonder?*

Sophie: *Erm, well, we don't or didn't really talk about things like that. I remember the fighting – it wasn't good. But it was okay. And then one day my dad left. I didn't speak to him for some years after that. But, you know, we speak now and it's okay.*

Louise: *I think that sounds like quite a big deal, you know. Must've been a confusing time for you.*

Sophie: *Yeah. (laughs)*

Louise: *How do you feel, thinking about it now?*

Sophie: *Erm, I feel a little bit nervous talking about it, actually.*

Louise: *Okay, thank you for telling me. How do you notice that you're feeling nervous?*

Sophie: *I feel a little bit dizzy, and my chest feels tight.*

This is a good example of how we often rationalise things from our past in our minds but our bodies tell a different story, acting as a thermometer to indicate that there may be something unresolved that needs attention.

Consider the following questions. As before, I'm looking for your initial gut reaction and then I want you to reflect on that reaction.

- Have you experienced any traumatic events?
- Have you ever been in a situation where you were afraid that you or someone else may die?
- Do you experience any recurring nightmares or flashbacks?

Now come back to anything that has come up from these questions. What impact do you think this has had on you? Some things to consider may be alcohol or drug use, your relationships with others, your sense of self-esteem, your successes and achievements, your fears, etc.

Now I want you to ask yourself: what could be perpetuating the impact of these events? In infertility, a perpetuating factor would be something like googling. Many of us turn to Google because it may seem as though it helps us to understand things. After all, as humans we are sense-making machines. We want to understand, we want to hear stories of hope, to feel as though we're not alone. BUT...! Googling obsessively can work against you because it means the mind never gets the opportunity to rest and repair – you simply get even more information that leads you further down a rabbit hole.

I'm not saying don't do your research, but I am saying be intentional, be aware. Of course, we're not just thinking about fertility trauma here, so let's look back to any past trauma and consider what you may be doing that is inadvertently perpetuating it.

At this point your inner fertility therapist is asking the patient (you), "What else do I need to know? What have we not covered yet? What might we have missed? What can help me (your inner fertility therapist) to help you?" So let's see if we can tease out any more.

- Are you generally being hard on yourself?
- Are you something of a perfectionist?
- Do you experience feelings of low self-esteem?
- Do you have a fear of failure?
- Where did these all come from?

Now think about your relationships:
- Who are you close to?
- Who supports you?
- Who is in your social network?
- Who knows you're working through this workbook?
- What significant relationships have there been in your story?
- What role do you play in your relationships?
- Do you have a partner? If yes, how is your relationship? If you don't have a partner, how do you feel about that?

Now think about this:
- What are your goals?
- What would you most like to see change in your day-to-day life?

Of course, the reason you're working through this workbook is that you want a baby. That's the big picture. But you don't decide you're going to summit Everest on the spur of the moment and achieve it the next day. It's a process of small steps. One small step I'd like you to consider is how you can facilitate a bit of time every day that ISN'T about fertility. This small step could very well be a step in the right direction.

Next, think about your happiness. How would we know you felt happy? When was the last time you felt happy? *Really happy?* That's a good question for anyone, not just around fertility. It's all about drawing stuff out. We all get caught in the rat race and it's easy to never stop and think "Am I *really* happy?" We ask ourselves if we've eaten enough, if we've had enough water, but do we ever stop and ask ourselves "Am I happy?"

What is happiness anyway? How would we know? What would change or shift your happiness level, aside from having a baby?

The more you ask these kinds of questions, the better you'll become at being your own therapist, at challenging yourself and being able to spot any changes in your thermometer. Let's see what this looked like when I worked with Brenda:

Louise: *Can you tell me about a time you felt happy?*
Brenda: *Happy? Um, gosh, happy. I am a happy person! I feel happy most of the time!*

Louise: *That's great! And how do you know that, would you say? How do you know when you are feeling happy?*

(At this point Brenda really reflected on the question and started to become a little agitated.)

Brenda: *So weird, I just don't even think about it! I felt happy at my wedding! I remember feeling happy then – I mean, I was stressed, but I was happy.*

Louise: *It looks like you're feeling a little stressed right now…*

Brenda: *Ha ha – maybe a little. You know, thinking about it now, I haven't felt happy for a while now. I mean, I am happy! I'm all right! I haven't laughed for a while. I haven't been able to make time to see my friends. I see my family – they make me happy. But then they ask about pregnancy et cetera, and I don't feel happy again. It's sort of like – I am cutting myself off from people, in case they ask. So I don't risk it. But then I feel a bit isolated. Oh God – you've got me thinking now.*

See how we make assumptions about how we are? But when we explore ourselves we find out so much more. When we add conscious awareness to something, it can disrupt the narrative. It gives us a more complete picture.

Now let's think about your physical health. How are you physically? I ask this question because I always approach this from a psychosomatic perspective. As we've discussed earlier, what's happening in your body could well reflect what is happening in your mind that isn't being addressed. Likewise with drugs and alcohol. If you have a history with alcohol or drugs, let's hear it – it's a part of your narrative. You might be unlikely to be using drugs and alcohol while trying for a baby, but have you in the past? What's the change been like? How did you navigate that? We're not asking this question to create shame but to understand more. If we didn't ask this question, it's as though we're negating it.

Exercise 5: Brief life history and timeline

Most of us understand that who we are as individuals is part nature and part nurture. This incredibly important exercise is focused on the nurture part – what has been put 'into' you through your experiences and conditioning. So, to kick this off, I'd like you to write down your earliest childhood memory.

....

....

....

....

....

....

....

....

Now let's consider what you recalled and wrote down. What does your inner therapist think about that? Why did that particular memory come to mind first? Was it a happy memory?

So much of who you are is created in your formative years. The genesis of your story starts with your parents and their parents. So let's explore that, starting with your mother:

- What was your mother like?

....

....

- What do you know about her background?

....

....

....

Now repeat these questions for your father and both sets of your grandparents. Having done that, now consider these further questions:

- What was your parents' fertility history? Easy pregnancy? Difficult delivery?

....

....

....

- What did you see of your mother and father's relationship?

....

....

....

- What about any siblings you may have?

....

....

....

....

- Where were you in the order of siblings?

....
....
....

- How did you get on with your siblings?

....
....
....

- What was your experience of school like?

....
....
....

- Did you enjoy school?

....
....
....

- What were you like at school?

....
....
....

- How was university/college?

....

....

....

- What other people were significant to you during your childhood?

....

....

....

Having thought about all the elements from your formative years, we need to get them organised in a timeline.

This exercise is somewhat about organising your memories in the right sequence, but the main purpose of it is to move your energy. We're aiming to use this as another tool to bring your unconscious memories and emotions to a conscious level. Writing things down, as we've discussed, is a great way to move that energy.

I'd like you to put the year you were born on the left and the current year on the right. Having done that, I need you to draw and label significant points in your life at approximately the right place on the timeline. Don't worry about being precise here – this is about moving the events on to paper. If you remember something else and need to fit it in, please add it either by adding a new line above or below the line.

YOUR TIME-LINE

Fill out your time-line below in the blank spaces with
significant events for each stage in your life

For now, I want you to just leave this here. We'll need this later when we're calibrating your authentic mindset at the end of the workbook.

Consolidation

Thank you for committing to do this. To really scrutinise and analyse yourself is not easy.

- What feelings are you left with?
- What stands out for you?
- What seems important?
- Were you surprised by anything?
- Were you more emotional about something than you thought you would be?
- Did you or your buddy learn something new about you?

I'd love to hear this but I'm entrusting you to hold onto it, to be kind with it and to use it in the way it's meant to be used. Use it to learn about yourself and draw out information in a non-judgemental way. Now have a break before you go on to the next chapter – what you have done here is a big deal.

Chapter 6

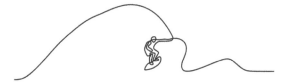

*Your Infertility
Anxieties:
From Fear to
Maternity*

In this chapter we're going to explore what makes you anxious, what this may mean and what we can do about it in terms of unblocking and clearing your way to your authentic mindset.

Anxiety is clever. It is sneaky. It can manifest in many forms and it can attach to many different worries or fears. It's our job, you and I, to be curious about what makes you anxious and what this anxiety can tell us.

While working with my patients, I learn not only from listening to what they say but also from what their body (a conduit of their unconscious) is telling me as they talk. I try to observe whether their body seems to agree with what they are saying or whether it seems to want to tell me something else. I do this by looking for what I like to describe as small 'discharges of anxiety', such as a flushed neck or chest. In some cases there may be an unconscious attempt to soothe this, such as touching the face or hair.

One time I remember sitting with my own therapist. He asked me how I felt about something and, as the conscious part of me answered in one way, the unconscious part of me betrayed me (or actually helped me) by discharging my anxiety through my feet, which had involuntarily started tapping. My therapist and I both noticed this, and through this 'tell' we knew that we weren't quite at the core of the truth. This display of mine led us to think together about what else could be going on.

It's through adopting this process of active listening that we can start to work out what may be living at the core of your anxieties and then, with hope, bring about healing.

So I want you to listen to yourself and discover what makes you feel anxious. Then we're going to work towards decreasing your anxiety. Without doubt, reducing anxiety makes life easier, but the added bonus for us is that it is wildly good for bringing down stress levels.

Remember what we said about stress? Stress leads to the production and spread of stress hormones throughout your body, and these surging stress hormones inevitably lead to inflammation. Inflammation feeds autoimmune problems, of which infertility is one.

We have to break this anxiety/stress hormones/autoimmune cycle, and we're going to do it by working through the anxiety and stress-related exercises in this chapter. By doing this work together, we are going to be able to give your body and mind some respite and naturally move you a step closer to your baby mindset.

One of the best ways to handle an episode of anxiety is through mindfulness. I showed you some mindfulness exercises earlier. However, unless there is an awareness regarding its drivers, then your anxiety will continue to manifest itself. So let's make it our job to work on this.

Before we get going, let's kick this process off with a quick anxiety check. How are you feeling right now, holding this workbook in your hands, in this very instant? It's important that you go with your gut reaction to each of the following statements. Don't overthink them. Even more importantly, pay attention to your body as you answer each one.

Tick whichever box you instinctively feel is closest to the 'real' you feel right now:

	Never	Rarely	Sometimes	Often	Very Often
I find it very hard to be at peace with myself and the world					
I have problems with my tummy					
I have a very short fuse and can quickly become angry					
I have felt light-headed on a few occasions					
I find it difficult to get to sleep					
I have feelings of being overwhelmed					
I have feelings of nervous tension					
I have feelings of dread					
I have had shaking hands					
I am always worrying					

Now have a look at your ticks and score them as follows.

Never	=	0
Rarely	=	1
Sometimes	=	2
Often	=	3
Very often	=	4

So what was your total?

0–10	It's unlikely you're suffering with anxiety.
11–26	You may be suffering from anxiety.
27–40	It's highly likely you're suffering from anxiety.

Now I want you ask yourself: how does seeing your score make you feel? Did your score surprise you? Did it annoy you? How does your body feel at this moment?

I'm going to ask you again to think about anxiety – about your anxiety. If you were to go and speak to a therapist today, what would you tell them was worrying you the most? What do you feel you would need them to hear? Tell your **inner** fertility therapist what you need them to hear now.

In this chapter I want you to learn how to move towards your anxiety. This is hard. Anxiety feels awful, and yet the more we avoid it, the more power it has over us. So let's confront it and let's start to chip away at its power. Are you in? Good. Listen up. This is probably the single most important thing I will tell you in this chapter.

Anxiety, when it's pronounced, is a defence against feeling.

Anxiety is one of the first markers that there is an emotion that feels too painful for you to go towards. A lot of the fertility patients I see are suffering a tremendous amount of grief and loss – so much so that they often feel as if getting close to that grief would be overwhelming and unrecoverable. So they do their best to avoid it. Quite often this means relentlessly undergoing medical interventions, cycle after cycle. Over time this can accumulate into anxiety, despair and hopelessness, because (and this is the second most important thing I will tell you in this chapter):

When you 'shut down' or avoid one type of feeling, you automatically shut them all down.

Unfortunately for us, it's not possible to selectively switch off 'negative' emotions such as loss and anger. When we consciously attempt to switch off one, the rest all follow. What this means is that, inadvertently, you switch off joy, happiness and hopefulness. The loss of these positive emotions is, in effect, collateral damage from the act of attempting to shut down your negative emotions.

So anxiety is one of the key markers we look for when trying to work out what feelings feel too overwhelming to get close to. Closely aligned with anxiety are its associated defence mechanisms. You may recognise these as coping strategies. Let's take a moment to consider them.

Your defences

We've all heard about defence mechanisms, right? So let's think about what yours might be. Identifying your automatic defences allows us to work out when and why they are being deployed and to start to work towards healing. More often than not, these defence mechanisms are unconscious – you won't necessarily even know you are deploying your agents of self-protection. As a result, we must be even more attuned to you, your body and what it feels like it must defend against.

Defence mechanisms are normal and are often healthy. However, in cases of trauma it's often these defence mechanisms that bring people to therapy. Once the defence is in place it does a great job of protecting us, but before long it begins to work against us, causing anxiety.

As joint fertility therapists on this journey, I want us to work out how you operate on a daily basis to defend against what you may not want to feel. To get things going, I've put together a list of some of the common defences I see when I work with my patients. Take a moment to read and consider them individually. There may well be some that are familiar to you.

- *Intellectualising*: thinking about feelings rather than 'feeling' them.
- *Suppression*: 'I will keep going!'
- *Denial*: 'I'm fine!'
- *Projection*: taking unwanted feelings and attributing them to someone else.
- *Displacement*: frustration at a partner/boss/parent taken out on someone else, e.g. kicking a pet (I know you would never do that!).
- *Sublimation*: e.g. channelling aggression into sports.
- *Rationalisation*: finding a reason for a situation we find hard to accept, e.g. it's God's will.
- *Reaction formation*: beyond denial, behaving in the opposite way to how you actually feel, e.g. extreme homophobes are quite often homosexuals.
- *Avoidance*: not classically a defence, but something we all do.

There are, of course, many more, but for now I'd like you to have a look at this list and identify which one resonates most with you. I also want you to observe yourself in day-to-day life and notice when these might come into play. When they do, give some thought to what they are trying to defend you against.

We can also learn a lot from the emotions that you *are* able to come into contact with. In infertility the resounding emotions, sadly, are guilt, shame and feeling like a failure. These are extremely difficult and upsetting emotions. And the worst part is that they work as a catalyst not only to feed your anxiety but to maintain their associated negative emotions, such as despair and hopelessness. We'll talk more about how to deal with these in Chapter 9 which considers grief and loss, but let me tell you now: the antidote to your anxiety and negative emotions is self-directed kindness, compassion and care.

So have you worked out the feelings that you *can* get into contact with? What are they? That's great. What we are after now are those feelings that you *can't* get in touch with. What is it that you are working so hard to defend against? Let's work it out. These are the feelings that make your feet start tapping or cause your breathing to become shallower. What has your body got to say about all of this? When we rule out what you *can* feel, then we shift our focus to listening to what might be more difficult to feel. Finding these feelings means digging deeper than the things we notice on the surface.

Quite often, patients I work with will observe, "You know, I feel ashamed of that," or they may suddenly ask, "Why is my body feeling anxious all of a sudden? Do I feel angry about that as well?" I'd like you to also be curious and to start questioning. The feelings you cannot get in contact with so easily might be more deeply hidden. These are the ones we need to work together to reach and unblock.

Ideally I'd like you to complete this next exercise with your buddy. They might find that asking you questions that explore your previous answers will take you into the deeper foundations of your feelings. If you're interested, this is known as Socratic questioning. The idea behind this method is to help you draw out how you may be feeling. Here are some examples to help you to get started:

Clarification	What do you mean when you say X? Could you explain that point further? Can you provide an example?
Challenging assumptions	Is there a different point of view? What assumptions are we making here? Are you saying that…?
Evidence and reasoning	Can you provide an example that supports what you are saying? Can we validate that evidence? Do we have all the information we need?
Alternative viewpoints	Are there alternative viewpoints? How could someone else respond, and why?
Implications and consequences	How would this affect someone? What are the long-term implications of this?
Challenging the question	What do you think was important about that question? What would have been a better question to ask?

While doing the following exercise, you might not notice anything at all – but your buddy might. I want them to pay close attention to you and look for any subtle signs that your body is reacting. Then I want them to pick up on them and ask you, "Hey – what just happened then?" That's when you should take a moment and work out whether your body reacted.

Quite often this reaction manifests as a sort of restlessness. Some patients feel jittery or have a sudden feeling of wanting to move away from some part of their body. Sometimes they might feel hotter or their heart rate might pick up a little. They might experience sweaty palms or movements in their arms or legs. What did your buddy notice?

Exercise 1: Childhood memory

I'm starting you off with a nice easy one. What is another early childhood memory? Get your buddy or your inner fertility therapist to really work through this with you using the Socratic questioning above.

I remember a patient who came to see me after struggling with anxiety and depression for ten years. TEN YEARS! Together he and I were struggling to work out what he was feeling as he told me that he felt nothing at all and said he could remember very little from his childhood. I would ask him question after question, like a detective of his unconscious, but repeatedly he would tell me he felt nothing. Then one day I noticed that as I asked him specific questions, his left hand was moving ever so slightly. It was only a tiny twitch of a movement. On certain questions there was no movement but on others his hand would twitch. In this way, his hand movement was a very discrete discharge of anxiety, and it provided me with a signpost towards what he was feeling and what was causing his anxiety and depression. This was the 'tell' I needed to help him dissolve the anxiety and depression that had taken over his life. His body helped me to help him. Much like I did then, I want you and your buddy to pay close attention for the tiniest of clues.

As I said, it's important to work through these questions either with your buddy or by writing your thoughts down. Simply thinking them through will not do the trick. So, going back to the original question: if you were to see a therapist today, what would you tell them about how you were feeling?

A little more on anxiety

We have to work to truly understand what is causing your anxiety. What in your unconscious is causing your body to react in a certain way? Yes, anxiety is normal and it will pass, but let's deepen our understanding. Let's understand *why* you are anxious. In that way, when we understand it, we can move it. Let's have a look at what anxiety can look like in infertility.

Tokophobia – an unspoken fear

With so many of my patients there is often an intense anxiety around childbirth and, to a lesser extent, pregnancy itself. Tokophobia is the fear of childbirth, from the Greek *toketós* (childbirth) and *fóvos* (fear of). In my experience, tokophobia and the anxiety that it creates are very often overlooked by the medical profession. I believe it's because we overlook it ourselves. "Pregnancy and a baby are all I want – how could I possibly be frightened of it?" Well, this is called conflict. But it's not spoken of, either because of the fear of being judged or because we believe that giving voice to a fear might somehow make it real.

So how do we begin to tackle a situation in which the thing you desire the most is the very thing that causes you so much anxiety? Sometimes a patient is battling tokophobia so much that it doesn't even register with them at a conscious level. When this is the case, we have to work through it together in order to give voice to their fear. It's only by processing the fear in this way that we can overcome it.

Very often the anxiety my patients feel doesn't register consciously with them because they are simply not talking about it. What you'll hear about in the following examples is the very common conflict between fear and desire. As I mentioned earlier in this workbook, for years you told yourself not to get pregnant. You may well have also convinced yourself that labour and childbirth would be terrifying, because sometimes it is! Let's take a closer look at what's going on with some of my other patients. These examples may well guide you to some insights of your own. Here is an excerpt from when I worked with Astra:

> **Louise:** *How do you feel about actually giving birth?*
> **Astra:** *Giving birth? That idea… Yikes. Makes me shudder… It will be worth it, though, I'm sure.*

What this told me was that Astra felt that the baby she wanted made her anxious, to the point where she would shudder. She physically shuddered as she spoke of the thought of childbirth. Her entire body displayed her unconscious fear. Why was something she wanted so much juxtaposed with anxiety? And why was she so confident that, despite this anxiety making her 'shudder', she could shake it off, that it would 'all be worth it in the end'? Her desire for a baby was in conflict with her thoughts about giving birth. Can you relate to this in any way?

Tokophobia is more common than you might imagine. Alex was another patient who was mentally wrestling with mixed feelings:

> **Louise:** *How do you think labour will be?*
> **Alex:** *It's tough, long and stressful, I'm sure. But I would also hope a happy time – as I have something exciting to look forward to.*
> **Louise:** *It feels like you've been thinking about labour quite a bit. Are you worried about it on the day?*
> **Alex:** *I worry I will be a hormonal bitch, I will get sick, I could die during childbirth, I could miscarry, I will have no energy, I will get fat, get stretch marks, I will get hairy.*
> **Louise:** *Okay, there's a lot there, isn't there, Alex?*
> **Alex:** *Yeah, but it's fine.*
> **Louise:** *Yes?*
> **Alex:** *Well, yeah, 'cause the pregnant me is happier than I've ever known, more excited than I've ever felt in my whole life, but at the same time more terrified than I've ever felt before.*

See what I mean? Alex is struggling with worries around childbirth. She's happy – content even – with being pregnant. It's just the bit at the end that she's anxious about. But when I watched her, I could see her body becoming agitated and restless as her anxiety increased. If we looked at her language alone you could see these as quite rational worries, but her body told me something else.

Now let's see what happened when I spoke with Jude. She was struggling with an internal conflict between the baby she wanted and some real unease around pregnancy. At the time we worked together, Jude was undergoing her first cycle of IVF treatment.

> **Louise:** *Okay, Jude, what's on your mind?*
> **Jude:** *I'm actually quite frightened by the prospect of it.*
> **Louise:** *You mean pregnancy in general or giving birth?*
> **Jude:** *Pregnancy – I guess I feel myself trying to dismiss my worries and concerns and any negative feelings I have towards it. I hope that if I do get pregnant it will feel natural and like it's meant to be and I'll embrace the changes to my body and to my lifestyle.*

Louise: *What sort of negative feelings are you trying to dismiss?*

Jude: *Well, being pregnant is obviously difficult because of the physical problems, pain, lifestyle changes, and it's inhibiting, maybe. But at the same time, I imagine the pain and suffering is counteracted by the fact that you have created a life.*

Louise: *I hear you. There's a lot of fear in this that perhaps we should look at and think about together.*

Jude: *You're right, of course there are the more unpleasant physical aspects and inconveniences, but predominantly I know that the love I develop for the child while I am pregnant, and knowing I am taking care of him or her in the best way I can, will outweigh any negative pregnancy symptoms.*

Rereading this, what's without doubt to me is that while pregnancy and childbirth can be a wonderful experience for some women, it can be full of difficulties and even a danger to their health for others. The views around both aspects seem to vary significantly between women. Please understand that I'm not trying to downplay any anxieties you may have – they may well be completely justified. But it is helpful to understand where your fears come from when it comes to pregnancy and childbirth. So let me ask you to think about the following:

- How do you think you will feel when you are pregnant?

....

....

....

- How do you think you will look when you're pregnant?

....

....

....

- What do you think your own labour and childbirth will be like?

....

....

....

Some women I have worked with see themselves as something of an Earth Mother and enjoy the state of being pregnant. Others have told me that they felt like a 'beached whale' and hated every moment of it. In reality, very few women experience no worries or fears whatsoever surrounding pregnancy and childbirth, and for some the thought of pushing a human being out is absolutely terrifying.

For a lot of the women I see, they feel that the reason they can't get pregnant is because everything that could go wrong has gone wrong. *Therefore, the birth will go wrong.* Does this resonate? If it does then we need to talk about it, to take the power out of it, because the more you keep it inside and suppress it, the more it breeds and intensifies.

One woman I worked with had suffered from terrible period pains and heavy bleeding from around the age of eleven. At the time there was shame and embarrassment attached to this, so she never talked about it. Later she applied the same rationale to her fears of childbirth, which were internally causing a great deal of anxiety.

She had been through lots of infertility treatment, but she had a terrible fear of childbirth and bleeding that she couldn't talk about because she was so embarrassed. It was the fact that she was unable to talk about it that we discovered together; and once we were able to get her to vocalise this fear, it was diminished. It was like shining a light under the bed to prove there are no demons lurking under there. Once the light is shone onto the perceived problem, its power is removed.

Let's have a look at how you feel about childbirth. Here are some questions that a therapist may typically ask when assessing a possible phobia:

- Do you have nightmares about the birth?

....

....

....

- Are you unable to feel the joy of pregnancy as your thoughts are preoccupied by the birth?

....

....

....

- Are you noticing any physical symptoms when people ask you about the birth?

....

....

....

- Have you considered harming yourself or terminating the pregnancy?

....

....

....

- Have you ever found yourself wishing you hadn't become pregnant?

....

....

....

- Do you feel as though this problem is so big that no one can help?

....

....

....

- Are you preoccupied by your thoughts about the birth?

....

....

....

- Are you finding that you avoid making a birthing plan?

....

....

....

- Do you feel afraid that you may panic when the time comes?

....

....

....

- Is your fear affecting your relationship or sex life?

....

....

....

- Is it interfering with your diet or physical activities?

....

....

....

- Does it affect your work or your sleep?

....

....

....

You might find that you answer "Yes" to some of these questions, suggesting that you have an element of fear around childbirth. Guess what? That's normal! But if you find that these questions really provoke your anxiety then it's vital that you speak to a fertility psychologist to help with this. Please visit www.conceivingconception.com to find a list of approved therapists. There is no shame, and it can be worked through.

Secondary infertility

I come across cases of secondary infertility surprisingly often (when you struggle to conceive following an earlier trouble-free pregnancy). Easily half the people I work with are suffering with it. Of those women suffering with secondary infertility, nine times out of ten it has its roots in some prior traumatic event, usually the effects of PTSD caused by a difficult first birth. Most women will 'forget' the pain of childbirth when they're flooded with happy chemicals from meeting their baby, but if you had a traumatic birth, especially one where you nearly died, your unconscious probably hasn't forgotten the pain. Let's consider some examples from those I have worked with before.

One patient I worked with had suffered a very traumatic experience: she nearly died while giving birth to her first child. As soon as she and her husband started talking about having another baby, she didn't want to have sex with him – in fact, she was furious with him. She simply couldn't get pregnant, because she was battling with unresolved PTSD. She had also found it hard to bond with her first child, because the birth nearly killed her. Let's take a look at how I worked through this with Peta:

> **Louise:** *Peta, I wanted to check in with you and see how you may feel about going through the story of the birth. How do you feel about that?*
> **Peta:** *Yes, okay.*
> **Louise:** *I've noticed that you have started to look a little anxious.*
> **Peta:** *Yes, but it's okay. I know we have to do this.*
> **Louise:** *Well, you are very brave, Peta, but we don't have to do anything. As we can see, just thinking about talking through it creates a reaction. Can you tell me about what is going on for you right now? What's happening in your body?*
> **Peta:** *I, um, I feel some pressure in my chest. I feel a little sort of fidgety in my legs and arms.*
> **Louise:** *And your breathing – how does that feel?*

Peta: *Feels a bit shallow? Maybe?*

Louise: *I see that. I wonder if we could take a few deep breaths together? Like we have done before?*

Peta: *Okay.*

Louise: *So if we breathe in for four seconds, hold it for seven seconds, and then big exhale for eight seconds. Let's just do a couple of these.*

Peta: *Yes.*

Louise: *Okay, so if we check in now, how are you feeling, Peta?*

Peta: *I feel a bit better. There's still some tightness in my chest.*

Louise: *Okay, thank you for letting me know. Does it feel okay to carry on? I think it would be good for us to understand what may be happening.*

Peta: *I always feel like this when anyone mentions the birth and what happened. (starts to cry)*

Louise: *I hear you. It sounds like it was very scary for you and for Jon.*

Peta: *Mm-hmm.*

Louise: *Let's just slow this down a little, and let's pay attention to what happens when you think about the birth of your daughter. I would like to let you know that you are experiencing a trauma response. You've gone into the stress response, fight-flight-freeze, like we discussed before. You sort of experience the trauma that has now passed, as though it is happening in the present.*

Peta: *Well, that's how it feels.*

Louise: *I hear you. So what we need to let you know is that this is a memory. You are safe. This is in the past.*

Peta: *Yes.*

Louise: *So we are going to check in with your body again. If we start with your head and move down, noticing how each part feels?*

Peta: *Head feels okay, maybe some pressure in my jaw, neck and shoulders feel very tight, chest a little tight, arms and legs okay now.*

Louise: *And your tummy? How does that feel?*

Peta: *Actually, a little like it has butterflies…*

Louise: *Okay, good to notice. Can you just check your breathing for me?*

Peta: *I keep forgetting that!*

Louise: *That's okay. Let's remember to both pay attention to your breathing.*

Peta: *Okay.*

Louise: *So if I can ask you again, how do you feel about telling me what happened when you went into labour and then what happened at the birth?*

Peta: *I feel okay about it.*

Louise: *Okay, so let's take this slowly, remember to breathe and remember this is a memory, it's in the past and you are safe.*

Peta told me that she was in labour for over twenty-four hours when the baby went into distress and she had to be rushed in for an emergency caesarean. At that time Peta was also haemorrhaging, and she remembers everyone around her panicking. She told me that she remembered looking at her partner's face and not understanding why he looked so terrified. It transpired that Peta was in respiratory arrest soon after, and they told her afterwards that they had very nearly lost her.

Peta recovered, despite being very uncomfortable and weak for several days. She remembered wanting so much to feel a 'bond' with her daughter, but that it didn't come naturally. It was as though, as much as she didn't want to, she blamed her daughter for 'nearly killing her'. Ashamed of feeling this way, she told no one. As time passed, her bond strengthened with her daughter and they developed a loving relationship. But Peta was unable to talk about the birth, and wished it away into the past.

After a few years, Peta and her partner began talking about a second baby. It was at this time that Peta started experiencing panic attacks. She also found herself avoiding sex with her husband, and felt herself starting to build resentment toward him. And although they were trying for over a year, she wasn't falling pregnant. Peta couldn't make sense of this; she wanted another child – that was what her family was supposed to look like – but she found her actions were betraying her intentions.

Talking all of this through, we identified PTSD. Peta was traumatised by the near-death experience she suffered when she was giving birth. When we worked through this trauma and we were able to tell the story without her experiencing a stress response, we overcame her PTSD.

Now we see the anxiety, what do we do with all of this? Well, the idea is that once we have identified what is at the core of your anxiety, the anxiety itself will significantly decrease. However, as we said earlier in the chapter, anxiety is sneaky. It works like a parasite, transferring and attaching itself to different parts of *your* life until the core of it has been processed and healed.

This will be a work in progress – it's not going to happen overnight. If you are also going through some form of infertility treatment, whatever that may look like, it's understandable that you feel anxious. So I would like us to have a look at some exercises we can do to help manage your anxiety, keep you grounded and make life feel a bit more manageable.

Anxiety has an appetite, and it wants to be fed

As I said, when you are trying for a baby, and especially when you have been trying for some time, it is very hard to make sense of things. I see this so clearly with unexplained infertility. It's hard to try to make sense of something that makes no sense. We are, after all, sense-making creatures – our minds are formed to understand and make sense of our surroundings. When things aren't going the way they should be, we automatically look for an explanation. However, what tends to happen is that this seeking of an explanation in an attempt to soothe the anxiety actually feeds it. Often this takes the form of googling and consuming as much data as is available on the Internet, looking for hope, looking for familiarity, looking for an explanation you can buy into.

Unfortunately, this doesn't work. Unless you are very disciplined with the amount of energy and time you give to this, you'll inevitably go on looking for the answer to one question and leave feeling worse about even more things that weren't even in your conscious mind. The tip here is to look for support as opposed to answers. By all means research. But when you notice your research tipping into obsessing, you must parent yourself and put in some restrictions. Anxiety loves data. It revels in it because it is a gateway to consuming your energy. Instead, I want you to focus your energy inwards. Imagine the amount of energy you put outwards, and instead send that energy towards yourself. I want you to do all that you can to bring your body and mind together. So instead of feeding anxiety, let's think of some alternative ways to cut it off at its source.

Control

When things aren't going the way we would like them to, we feel out of control. That's normal. Yet this seems magnified in infertility, especially if you have given your body over to medical professionals. So let's think about it this way. There are things in life that we can control and there are things in life that we cannot control. So we either choose to act or we choose not to act on the things we can or cannot control. When you can control something and you choose to act, that normally leads to a sense of achievement and satisfaction. But when you choose to act on things you *cannot* control, that leads to a feeling of frustration and anxiety.

Have a look at this matrix:

	Things I CAN control	Things I CAN'T control
I CHOOSE *TO* ACT		
I CHOOSE *NOT* TO ACT		

Look at each box and tell me what you think the outcome will be for each one. For example, if there is something in life you can control and you choose to act on it, what do you think will be the outcome? Will it be positive or negative?

Think about what you're in control of. Conversely, I also want you to think about what you are not in control of. If you identify something that you can control but you choose not to act on it (e.g. not use this workbook, not complete the journal, not check your temperature, not practise mindfulness), that's where you're in danger of adopting a 'victim' mindset. A victim mindset leads, inevitably, toward depression. So doesn't it make sense to take action and take control of the things you can control?

Now have a look at the completed table. The hardest box of all is when you cannot control something and you choose not to act – this means you're 'letting go', and it's the wisest place to be.

	Things I CAN control	Things I CAN'T control
I CHOOSE *TO* ACT	Achievement & satisfaction	Frustration
I CHOOSE *NOT* TO ACT	Victim	Wise judgement

Exercise 2: Your matrix of control

I'd like you to make a list here of the things you can control and the things you can't control. This will be helpful in highlighting where your energy is best spent and show you the path to our ideal place: wise judgement.

Things I can control

....

....

....

....

....

Things I can't control

....

....

....

....

....

If you're used to being in control and getting results, infertility can come as something of a shock to your system. When your fertility is not giving you the results you want, you tend to keep pushing harder and harder. The problem here is that, at the moment at least, your fertility is not something you are in control of.

If you feel that you're struggling with control and letting go, we need to work on keeping you in the present and grounding yourself. We will work on this together by using the mindfulness exercises from the earlier chapter, including the 5–4–3–2–1 Grounding Exercise.

Mindfulness is a way of befriending ourselves and our experience.
Jon Kabat-Zinn

Anxiety means you're not in the present. In fact, anxiety usually means that your mind is projecting you into the future, as it's borne out of the fear of something that may or may not happen. So if we can anchor or ground you in the present, we can learn to manage your anxiety. That's why the mindfulness exercises in Chapter 4 are so useful – they stop your mind from racing ahead and creating anxiety. Remember: your anxiety is hungry!

Let's think about the way we eat. Mindful eating, instead of just mindlessly eating (which we all do), means you make a real effort to slow down and contemplate every mouthful. It means thinking about every texture, noticing every smell, really looking at the colours. An easy way to start thinking about mindfulness is to eat mindfully. Eating is something we do all the time and pay no attention to. Funnily enough, I learned about mindful eating at school. We were each given a Malteser and we all had to think about it melting in our hands. We noticed the chocolate melting. What did it feel like in our mouths? How did it taste? What did it feel like as the chocolate melted away?

Mindfulness gives you a completely different appreciation for eating. It's about getting your mind out of 'autopilot' and into the actual experience. Did you know that Buddhist monks eat their first meal of the day in complete silence? By doing this without distractions of any sort, they calm their minds ready for the day. Again, mindfulness.

Exercise 3: Self-care

What do I mean by self-care? Well, I've noticed that many of the women I work with are very hard on themselves. You might also find that you beat yourself up because of the challenges you are facing around pregnancy. It's very easy to slip into a mindset that your body has somehow betrayed you or that your body now belongs to the medical professionals as some sort of experiment. At the same time, you're constantly bombarded with the sights, sounds and news of new lives that your friends and family have achieved – seemingly effortlessly. This mindset is counterproductive, and I want to share with you a few ways to adopt a more compassionate mindset. Trust me when I tell you it will pay you back in so many ways.

I'd like you to imagine compassion. When I ask people to do this, many of them naturally think of someone they know who is compassionate. But I'd urge you to try to think of an object or an image as opposed to a person you know. I want you to do that because, in reality, no one you know is perfect. So can you try? Take a moment and choose an image and hold it in your mind's eye. (If you're really struggling to think of anything other than a person, then please make that person absolutely the best they can possibly be, and endow them with the qualities that follow.)

Okay. Now you've settled on an image, I want you to associate some specific qualities with it.

- It needs to be understanding.
- It needs to be kind.
- It needs to be wise.
- It needs to be forgiving.

Now I need you to slow down. Take a moment. Breathe slowly and deeply. Pay attention to your breathing. Close your eyes and visualise your object (or person if you must) of compassion. Start to think about your image.

- What does it look like? Understand that it is kind, understanding, accepting of you and wise.
- How is it looking at you?
- How will it communicate with you?
- What does its voice sound like?
- Does it have a colour?

- How else can it interact with you? Touch?
- What does it want you to know and understand?
- What is it saying to you?
- While you spend time with it, how does it make you feel? What do you notice?

It's important that you know this compassionate image is unique to you. It is available for you whenever and wherever you need it – just slow down and bring it to mind if you feel yourself becoming anxious.

Exercise 4: Make a Compassionate Pack

Some of my patients find it helpful to assemble what I like to call a Compassionate Pack. Consider this as something of a 'break glass in emergency' pack that you know is there for you if you feel your anxieties starting to overwhelm you.

This pack is something physical, as opposed to the mental image I just asked you to conjure in your mind. It's a way of gathering things to remind you to be compassionate with yourself. My patients often tell me how simple and effective this can be for them, and I hope you find it helpful too. Life's journey is a long one, and we all need a little lift now and then. This Compassionate Pack should help.

Have a look around your home to find something you can use to hold a small collection of objects. This could be a small bag, a box or even some Tupperware. You get the idea – not cumbersome, but also not tiny either. It needs to be of a size that you can leave it somewhere visible so that it reminds you every day that it is there for you if you need it. Maybe it can sit by your bedside.

Now I want you to look for small objects that soothe, inspire or motivate you. This could be a photograph of a time when you felt really happy, or maybe a candle to remind you to relax. They should be items that remind you to take care of yourself. You get the idea – we're looking for things with positive associations.

Of course, as you hunt around, you may come across items that bring back some sad memories. I'll leave it to you to decide if they ought to go in your Compassionate Pack. Remember, you'll be using this in times of anxiety to soothe and ground you, so it's better to have several items rather than one big one. Don't worry if you struggle to gather more than a couple of items; just start small and add to your Compassionate Pack as you go along. What's important is that you start.

Once your pack is assembled (or started), keep it somewhere visible every day. Then if you start to feel yourself becoming overwhelmed, like it's all a bit too much, reach for your Compassionate Pack. This pack is your antidote to negative emotions, and the fact that you know it's there and you know how to use it should bring you comfort and reassurance.

Exercise 5: Your story

I've said it before, but it is worth repeating: what we're dealing with here is trauma. Think back to the assessment we did when I asked you if you'd experienced any traumatic events. Here I want to bring the trauma to mind so that we can talk about it.

Let me explain why with an example. When I work with my patients who are suffering with secondary infertility, all too often there was something traumatic about either the conception, the pregnancy, the birth or life after the first child had arrived that they simply didn't want to talk about. And the reason they didn't want to talk about it is that if they did, they would *feel* it.

But that's just the point. I need you to talk about it. I need you to feel it. I need you to talk and feel it over and over again, because it's only through bringing it all back to your conscious, to the surface, that you can deprive your anxiety of the fear – the fuel – that it needs to survive. It's only by talking about it repeatedly that you can extinguish the anxiety that it brings up today.

The part of the mind that is responsible for processing is called the prefrontal cortex. When a trauma occurs, our mind will often try to help us by making our prefrontal cortex stop working normally because it's all 'too much'. Essentially, it takes it offline. This inhibits the memory-forming process by preventing the information from travelling to the hippocampus to become a long-term memory.

The problem with this is that later on, when you mentally revisit the trauma, your amygdala (the fight-or-flight part of your mind) becomes activated and the traumatic event feels like it's happening right now. This is because the original event hasn't been processed in the normal way. The easiest way to get that processing part working again is to talk about the suppressed memory.

If you have memories of a traumatic episode (or episodes) associated with your last pregnancy, or indeed whatever may be coming up for you now, I want you to talk about them with your buddy. And as you tell the story, when you feel really anxious I want you to breathe and remind yourself that you are safe and this is just a memory.

Each time you start the story you may find yourself remembering more and more details that eluded you on the first telling. That's fine. In fact, that's good. You may still feel crushing anxiety on the second, third or even the fourth telling of the story, but I promise you that with each round of talking through the experiences, the anxiety will decrease. You may need to do this over a period of days, but I promise it will get better.

As you work through the repeated telling of this story you will, little by little, become desensitised to it. When you think you've cracked it with your buddy, I want you to practise telling it to other people in your social circle, such as friends and family members.

What is important here is your buddy. While it may seem logical to choose your significant other as your 'therapist' for this exercise, you need to think very carefully about it. When a fertility-related trauma has occurred, I often see that trauma ricocheting between partners. Through empathy the listening partner gets upset, and so the talking partner clams up so as to not upset them. But what you are trying so hard to do here is to talk about the trauma. So you need to choose your buddy wisely here. They need to be as neutral for this as a regular therapist would be. You're looking for someone who can mirror your pain but not add extra to it from their own experience. If it's not possible to find someone apart from your significant other to work through it with, then the exercise needs to be set up with some agreed rules about who will fill the neutral party role initially. You can take turns, each of you making the best effort to remain neutral for the other. This is difficult, but it's worth doing if your buddy is someone close to you.

I want you to keep telling this story until the point arrives where your mind says to your anxiety, "It's okay now. It happened, but it doesn't define who I am." It is only through talking about it that you will feel this. If you feel it and you allow those feelings (both conscious and unconscious) to be expressed, eventually the anxiety will not have anything to feed on any more. You're taking away any power it has over you, your life and your womb.

If you can't get to the point where you are able to work through this with someone, then the next best thing to do is to journal it. Once it's journaled, read it back to yourself. Then read it out loud to yourself. Then perhaps record yourself reading it and play it back to yourself. Again, I'm not saying this is easy, but it is an important thing to do.

Exercise 6: Journaling

Journaling encourages mindfulness and helps you to remain present while maintaining a sense of perspective. This helps you to control feelings of anxiety and generally improves your mood. Journaling also helps you to prioritise your concerns, fears and problems through the simple process of tracking them over time. By recording things daily, you become better equipped to spot your triggers and start to control them. A happy by-product of journaling is that it has been found to improve your confidence and sense of identity.

The best way to journal is simply to write. Put pen to paper and see what comes up. While there is no right or wrong way to journal, try to avoid the temptation to review and edit your writing. This is where you can just be yourself.

In all these exercises we are aiming to make your anxiety more manageable. So instead of your anxiety being unspoken, we want to think about it and write about it every day. By doing this we start to take the power out of it; we move its energy. Remember that anxiety gives us information, and information we can use is good – we can make this information work for us.

What is the difference between a good athlete and an 'elite' athlete? Does an elite athlete feel no nerves? Of course not. The biggest difference is that elite athletes have learned to turn their nerves into performance.

I'd like you to commit to writing your journal for at least a month.

This daily practice will help you to tune in to what is happening in the present moment. Once you increase your awareness, you will start to understand what triggers your anxiety, and once you know your triggers, you will be in a far better position to tackle them. Like I said, information is good. Information is your friend. So let's start gathering some information.

There's no right or wrong way to journal, but if it helps you to get going, I have provided an outline at the back of the workbook.

Finally, note here something that happened today that made you happy. I'd like you to focus on this for five minutes.

....

....

....

....

....

....

....

....

I have added more Journal pages at the back of the workbook for you to use. Please keep it up.

Consolidation

So now I've made you aware of your anxieties, I hope I have given you some tools to help you to manage them. Having worked through this chapter, and by continuing with your daily journal, you will start to feel less anxious, more contained and more aware. By increasing your awareness, we can wean you off any compulsive repetition that feeds your anxiety. As humans, we will repeat the same patterns over and over again until we make ourselves aware of them, so unless you bring awareness to the forefront of your mind through talking and examining your unconscious, you will keep doing the same thing over and over again. Let's break the cycle!

Chapter 7

Getting to Know your Baby: Making Room for Another

It is not inertia alone that is responsible for human relationships repeating themselves from case to case, indescribably monotonous and unrenewed: it is shyness before any sort of new, unforeseeable experience with which one does not think oneself able to cope. But only someone who is ready for everything, who excludes nothing, not even the most enigmatical will live the relation to another as something alive.

Rainer Maria Rilke

The quote above seems pretty deep, right? But it encapsulates what this chapter is about. Human relationships repeat themselves, and to break the patterns I'm going to ask you not to exclude this chapter. Why would you exclude it? Because the chances are that unless you've done anything like this before, you may think this chapter feels a bit 'out there'. But I want you to take a crash course in psychodynamic theory. I'll show you how.

Consider everything you've heard about therapy, 'psychobabble', the unconscious, Freud and the analyst's couch. I'm going to ask you to take a leap of faith with me here and try to get into that kind of frame of mind. I wonder if this will feel natural for you or perhaps a little arduous or abstract. Either way, if you can indulge me and stay with me, this is where the good stuff is. You're going to need all the skills you've learned so far so you can apply them to your unconscious and get your authentic mindset up and running.

While this chapter is important, I want you to have fun with it too. For me as a therapist, this is the most fascinating area and the one where I can begin to understand someone on a deep level.

When I was a psychology student, I had a mentor who was fantastic at identifying the unconscious and interpreting it. I remember once playing him a recording of a session I had done with a patient (when we train, we record with consent). At the very beginning the patient was telling me about some shoes and a shoe rack. I remember saying to my supervisor, "Oh, let me fast forward this bit and take us somewhere a bit more interesting," but he said, "No…this is everything – listen carefully." As I listened to what I thought was an empty and largely pointless monologue about a shoe rack that was at the patient's front door, I realised that she was describing herself as she described a particular pair of shoes that didn't seem to fit in the rack. She spoke about how the shoes didn't fit in with the way the rack looked. We later worked out that she was describing herself – *she* was the shoe. Her consciousness was talking about a pair of shoes and a shoe rack, but her unconscious was saying something different. Are you starting to see how this works? Often our conscious minds aren't quite yet able to comprehend what is underlying at the unconscious level. Consequently, it falls to the therapist to 'catch' it. I want to show you how to catch it yourself.

If I ask you what the ink blot below looks like, what's the first thing that comes to mind? Don't think about it too much – this is your unconscious coming through. This chapter is all about going with the flow.

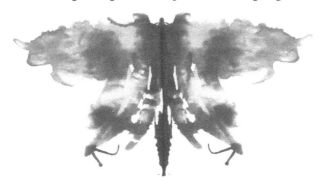

So what do you see here?

....

....

....

....

....

Of course, there is no right or wrong answer – you just need to go with it. For this chapter, it doesn't really matter what your reality is. Reality is whatever you say it is.

When we do the exercises in this chapter, I want you to make every effort to shut out any judgement. If you do find yourself judging your answers or thinking they sound crazy, stupid or simply nonsensical, then we won't get very far. I urge you to embrace free association. Non-judgemental and open – that's where we need our minds to be.

So let's try this out.

Exercise 1: The sinking ship

In this first exercise I have used the word 'mother', but you should feel free to substitute it for the most significant person from your formative years.

I want you to imagine that you and your mother are on board a ship and it's about to sink. At the very last moment a lifeboat comes along. However, there is only one seat available. This means that only one of you can be saved.

So…who gets the seat?

....

Now, what did you notice? Write your observations here.

....

....

....

Now let's try this again, but this time you are on the boat with the child you're trying for. Who gets the seat then?

Now, what did you notice? Write your observations here.

....

....

....

Now, I'm not generally inclined to gamble but I'd hazard a guess that for the second scenario you answered 'your child'.

Did you?

In the second example, your desire to save your child is instinctive. It's a given. It's a truly visceral and natural thing to do. And yet so many people I work with buck this natural order of things in the first scenario and choose to take the seat themselves. So what's going on here?

As much as we can argue cases for who gets saved, and as much as it is not very pleasant to think of a parent not being saved, if you sacrificed yourself to save your parent in the first scenario then we may need to think about the dynamics you have with that parent.

So what does this mean? Through visualisations and imagination, we can start listening to your unconscious mind. This is called thinking psychodynamically.

Psychodynamics

The psychodynamic model of therapy all started with Sigmund Freud. Understanding this aspect of therapy will give us another method of unblocking your way towards your all-important authentic mindset – one that is not inhibited by your unconscious.

Psychodynamic therapy looks at the dynamics in our internal world (how we relate to ourselves and different parts of ourselves) and our external world (how we relate to the world around us and other people). There is a focus on understanding the links between past and present experiences.

Making sense of past experiences can help resolve conflicts within ourselves and in our relationships with others. The psychodynamic approach is sometimes referred to as 'uncovering therapy' because its aim is to look deeper into problems, to make what may have been unconscious conscious. It's arguably the most complex therapeutic approach, but I am confident we can get through this together.

Psychodynamic therapy assumes that chronic problems (what we call 'blocks') are rooted in the unconscious mind and must be brought to light for unblocking to occur. This is aligned with all the steps and techniques we have been working through in this workbook. We must have the self-awareness to discover these unconscious patterns of thought and get an understanding of how these patterns came to be in order to deal with them.

So we need to understand and acknowledge that our thinking and behaviour are affected by processes of which we are not fully conscious. The unconscious mind comprises mental processes that are inaccessible to our conscious mind but that influence judgements, feelings and behaviour. Here we can go back to our good friend Freud, who said, "The unconscious mind is the primary source of human behaviour." Much like the iceberg, the most important part of the mind is the part you cannot see.

This means that we unconsciously recreate patterns and behaviours. Interestingly, we see this in animals too. So, for example, if a monkey follows a path in the jungle and a coconut hits it on the head, you'd think it would take a different path next time it is out in the jungle. But it doesn't. It may take the same path, even though that path resulted in a bad experience. Just like humans, the monkey is unconsciously recreating a behaviour that is ultimately hurting it. Why? Because although the monkey *knows* that it got hurt last time it went that way, it is unconsciously trying to rectify the situation. It wants to try it again so that this time the situation might turn out differently. But by not consciously thinking about it, what's really happening is that the monkey keeps on getting hurt. This concept applies to us too.

Often, if you have a secure, healthy upbringing, that's what you will repeat: healthy, secure relationships. If you had an insecure, abusive or neglectful experience, you'll tend to repeat this familiar pattern in an unconscious attempt to resolve it. And it's highly likely that it will remain unresolved until the pattern is broken or until the part that we can't see just yet, because it's unconscious, is identified. The good news? We're going to find these patterns and behaviours by making you self-aware.

Mike had been with his partner, Tom, for fifteen years, and they were planning to marry two weeks after he started seeing me for therapy. He told me that he was unhappy in his relationship and that Tom was needy and controlling because he was frightened that Mike would abandon him.

Mike was good-looking, successful and confident, but somehow he prioritised Tom's fear of abandonment over his own happiness. Mike grew up with his mother, whom he said he loved very much. His father had separated from his mother while Mike was young, and Mike was initially dismissive of his father's place in the story. "That's all in the past," he said. "It's forgotten about and doesn't worry me."

> **Louise:** *What does Tom think about you coming to therapy?*
> **Mike:** *He doesn't know. I would never be able to tell him.*
> **Louise:** *Why not?*
> **Mike:** *Because he would think I was coming to talk about him.*
> **Louise:** *Why can't he know that?*
> **Mike:** *Because he would be frightened I was leaving him.*
> **Louise:** *And why can't he know that?*
> **Mike:** *He wouldn't be able to cope. It would destroy him.*
> **Louise:** *It sounds like staying with him is destroying you.*
> **Mike:** *Yeah, maybe, but it would be worse for him.*

Louise: *Why?*

Mike: *I don't know.*

Louise: *Mike, I wonder if it's because you know what it feels like for a man to leave you?*

Mike: *No, no. You mean my dad? That's got nothing to do with it. No. It can't be. I haven't even thought about him.*

Louise: *I hear you, Mike. But look at your body...you look as though you're having a very emotional reaction.*

Mike cried here, and it felt as though a huge emotional burden was lifted. This is a small excerpt from a much longer conversation, but do you see the link? The unconscious part of Mike that hadn't dealt with his father leaving him was keeping him from leaving a man that was making his life very unhappy. Once the block was removed, Mike was able to think about this relationship from a different and more conscious perspective.

What we're doing here is bringing to the fore what may have been a very faint thread from the past. We're turning the thread from a single strand into a rope that you must pull up because you must understand it, examine it, take it apart, keep going over it to take the power away from it. You may not get it right, but you're taking a chance. Don't let this risk put you off – your body will tell you if it's right. The following quote is so true:

> Between stimulus and response there is a space. In that space is our power to choose our response. In our response lies our growth and our freedom.
> *Viktor Frankl*

For Mike, initially the stimulus was his relationship, and his response was his remaining in it despite his knowledge that it didn't make him happy. There was no space, because everything was being held in the unconscious. When he came to see me, we changed the algorithm to include space. This space gave Mike the chance to reflect on his relationship from a conscious perspective. This is what we are trying to create; this is the space.

Parts (of the self)

If I said to you that we all have different parts to ourselves, what does that make you think?

Okay, now what does it make you *feel*? We are opening a dialogue with you here, but with the two different parts of you.

Let's put it like this: if you feel jealous or angry or upset when you hear the news of yet another pregnancy or birth, that's only a part of you reacting to it. It's okay to feel these emotions – they don't define you. It's just how you feel at that moment in time. Does that resonate? Without nurture and attention, these feelings can fester and become a part of ourselves that we feel compelled to banish.

It's like when I ask a patient about what their parents were like. They might say positive things, but when I ask them to explore their relationship more deeply I find a resistance. It could be they think that if they talk about someone negatively, people will think negatively of them, so they only portray the positive. But if we really think about it, everything in life has to be balanced. Without yin there would be no yang, without dark there would be no light, without love there would be no hate. Love and hate must coexist, to be held and equally integrated. For example, I love my partner but sometimes they get on my nerves. This is normal, because you can't just have the good bit all the time – life is *all* the bits, and this also applies to ourselves.

When we talk about the different parts of ourselves, we're talking about the different parts of our psyche that make up the whole. It's important here to think about the darker parts, often known as the 'shadow' part. A shadow is the dark part of our selves, the part that might secretly not be as politically correct as it 'should' be. But because we view that part of ourselves as 'bad', we deny it, we pretend it's not there. The result? It gets put into a box and hidden away. Carl Jung had a deep interest in the shadow and the process of assimilating "the thing a person has no wish to be" instead of hiding it away. Your shadow may be so well hidden that you're not even aware of it! Becoming familiar with your shadow is an essential part of the therapeutic process. It is a part of you, and we cannot look at you completely without looking at this critical part of your psyche. All these elements collectively make you more rounded, more whole and more colourful.

Exercise 2: Into the shadows

Why don't we have a try at accessing your shadow? It sounds ominous, doesn't it? But in the spirit of being open and non-judgemental, I want to ask you: what is the one thing that really gets your goat? What grinds your gears? What about people and society drives you mad?

Now, what did you notice? Write your thoughts here.

....

....

Here's how it went with a patient I had been working with:

> **Louise:** *You've been away? How was it?*
>
> **Jasmine:** *It was lovely! So nice to be away!*
>
> **Louise:** *Mmmm, great.*
>
> **Jasmine:** *Yes, it was great, but it was a bit of a shame as the beaches were covered in litter. People are just so irresponsible. (laughs)*
>
> **Louise:** *(sensing the laughter was diffusing something) Right.*
>
> **Jasmine:** *Made me feel a bit annoyed.*
>
> **Louise:** *Can you tell me about that?*
>
> **Jasmine:** *Well, yeah. I mean, urgh! Just litter everywhere, people not respecting the place, just taking the piss!*
>
> **Louise:** *Seems like you're feeling that annoyance just now?*
>
> **Jasmine:** *Yes, well, I am, actually. How would they feel if I just littered everywhere or did whatever I wanted to do?*
>
> **Louise:** *Well, we've talked about this before, haven't we? This sense of social responsibility and how it can make you feel frustrated and annoyed.*
>
> **Jasmine:** *Yes, it drives me mad!*
>
> **Louise:** *Well, you know what it reminds me of? It reminds me of how things are at home, with you being the responsible one, you doing everything with little help.*
>
> **Jasmine:** *Yeah.*
>
> **Louise:** *Well, I wonder if you are telling me about the litter and how it*

made you feel angry because it's easier than telling me that you are angry at your partner?

So did you spot the shadow part? The part that Jasmine judges as wrong, that gets denied in her consciousness but projected onto others in her unconsciousness? What she witnessed was certainly annoying, but it seemed to represent more than that. It's a way of identifying the shadow part and then working with that. Letting Jasmine know it was okay to be angry at her partner aided the work we were doing on her self-esteem and encouraged her to create better boundaries at home.

How does that apply to what we are doing?

Psychodynamic theories suggest that any wished-for child – not just pertaining to infertility – is a projection of our own unmet needs or desires or perhaps broken relationships. Professionally we would call this a transference receptacle.

We've all heard of projecting – the defence mechanism by which your ego defends itself against unconscious impulses or qualities (both positive and negative) by denying their existence in yourself and, instead, attributing them to others. In our current scenario, your wanted-for baby is the receptacle – or container – for these projections. Make sense? Stay with me, because if we can work out what this baby means to you, we may get some helpful information about what you are avoiding letting yourself feel 'consciously' but which may be blocking you 'unconsciously'.

Your wanted-for baby is not simply a projection of what you want in the future. It is coloured by everything that has happened in your past, including any unconscious images and feelings about yourself, your own parents and siblings, your partner and visions of your pregnancy and motherhood.

Let me give you an example. I was working with a woman who had a very pronounced fear that when she eventually had a baby, her partner might love the baby more than she did, leaving her feeling unwanted, rejected and left out:

Neeta: *I feel so embarrassed telling you this.*
Louise: *Do you? Why is that?*

Neeta: *It's just so stupid, but I think about it all the time.*

Louise: *Okay, well, take your time and tell me when you're ready. I'm not going to judge you, I'm here to listen and help you make sense of things.*

Neeta: *I am worried that my partner is going to love the baby more than me.*

Louise: *I understand. How did it feel saying it out loud?*

Neeta: *Like a relief!*

Louise: *I bet! So let's think about it. Why do you think he will love the baby more than you?*

Neeta: *I do not know! It's ridiculous.*

Louise: *Well, how does it make you feel when you think about it?*

Neeta: *It makes me feel really sad! Like I will be all alone or something. Like, rejected!*

Louise: *And what's that like? When you say you feel rejected?*

Neeta: *I hate it – makes me sad and really anxious.*

Louise: *And that feeling of rejection – do you remember feeling it before? In the past? Do you get a sense of when you may have felt rejected?*

Neeta: *Well, my mum always made me feel rejected. But that's different.*

Louise: *Does it feel okay to explore it a little?*

We then explored Neeta's relationship with her mother. I had gathered in the initial assessment that there was a difficult dynamic with her mother, but as we talked it through, Neeta made the link herself. I find that discovering connections for yourself helps to build your own sense of therapeutic autonomy, leading to (hopefully) the cultivation of your own inner therapist.

Neeta's mother had made her feel unwanted because she perceived that her father had loved Neeta more than he loved her. Now, I'm not saying here that if you work out your mother issues you'll get pregnant. But what I am saying is that Neeta, like many, was harbouring unconscious projections about her baby that were now outdated in the present. The hurt that Neeta's mother had caused her, which was never talked about, took its toll on Neeta's self-esteem and sense of self-worth. It was also being re-enacted in her current relationship: Jo simply assumed her partner would repeat what had happened in the past.

When you really start to investigate the unconscious you can work out that, in this example, Neeta's mother resented her because her father loved her more than he loved his wife. By following a similar approach, you can unlock what you may be projecting onto your wanted-for child. This means you can then heal any wounds that may have been created by a carer and which were out of your control.

So let's do that now. What are your thoughts, hopes and wishes for your baby? Equally, what are your fears and anxieties? Remember: you can be totally honest.

Write your answers here.

....

....

....

....

....

....

....

....

....

....

What do you make of this?

Bringing awareness to how and why we feel a certain way can free us from emotional baggage. It can help Neeta choose to have a child for her own reasons, not for reasons that were projected on to her. I believe that coming to that understanding takes away any unconscious anxiety. By taking away the anxiety, we're putting desire in control rather than fear.

Are you starting to see how this works? What's been going on for you as you've read this? What is happening between you and your therapeutic partner, or indeed, what is happening in all these parts of yourself? Remember to use the Socratic questioning method you have learned and use your own feelings as thermometers.

Exercise 3: The Cube Test

A Japanese psychologist by the name of Tadahiko Nagao developed a method of accessing the unconscious using a visualisation and a series of questions. He called it the Cube Test, and I'm going to guide you through my version of it here. It's important that you describe whatever comes to your mind first for each question. I also recommend writing your answers down so that it's easier to figure out your results at the end (and harder to waffle about your answers or change them for a result that you prefer).

Please follow these instructions in the order they are presented and try to be as honest as you can. Remember: no judgements.

I would like you to imagine that you are in a desert.

There's nothing around you but sand and space.

Now, in the desert you are going to see a cube.

Describe it to me. How big is it? What is it made of, and what is the surface like? What colour is it? Where in the desert is it? Where is the cube (e.g. on the ground, floating)? Is it transparent? If so, can you see inside?

Write your answers here.

....

....

....

....

....

Now I want you to think of a ladder. How long is this ladder, what's it made of, and where is this located in your desert? Where is it in relation to the cube?

Write your answers here.

....

....

....

....

....

Next you'll see a horse. Tell me about the horse. What colour is it? What is the horse doing, and where is it in relation to your cube?

Write your answers here.

....

....

....

....

....

Flowers are next. Where are the flowers in your desert and how many are there, and where are they in relation to the cube?

Write your answers here.

....

....

....

....

....

Finally, you are going to see a storm. Tell me about the storm. What do you see? What kind of storm do you see and what is the distance between the storm and the cube?

Write your answers here.

....

....

....

....

....

Now, before moving on to the interpretation of your vision, I want you to reimagine the entire scenario once more. Make sure that the image in your head is clear. Write it down if you haven't already, or even draw it if you want to.

Right. Now let's ask ourselves: what does it all mean? Don't worry about getting the right answer, as there isn't one. I've done this several times and never heard the same answer twice. So let's go.

The Cube

The cube represents you.

The cube is a symbolic version of how you view yourself and how you feel you are viewed by others. The size of the cube is a representation of your ego. Was your cube very big or perhaps very small? The surface of the cube represents what is visibly observable about your personality, or maybe it is what you want others to think about you. The texture of the cube could be representative of your nature. Where was your cube in relation to the sand? Was it grounded in the sand, flat or on an edge?

Note your interpretations here:

....

....

....

....

....

....

....

....

....

....

....

The Ladder

This represents friends and friendship.

The location and material of your ladder can also tell you how close you are with your friends. You guessed it – the closer the ladder is to the cube and the stronger the ladder is, the better it is for your friendships!

Note your interpretations here:

....

....

....

....

....

The Horse

The horse represents your ideal partner.

Was your horse playing and running around, or grazing right next to your cube? Perhaps it was further away? What do you think this means? How do you feel about how you described the appearance of the horse? Ring any bells?

Note your interpretations here:

....

....

....

....

....

The Flowers

Okay, this is a sensitive one, so take your time with it. The flowers represent children and family.

What did you notice about the flowers? How many were there? Where were they in relation to the cube? Think about their colour. It's okay to take a second and tune in with yourself on this one.

Note your interpretations here:

....

....

....

....

....

The Storm

The storm represents your fears.

Was the storm scary and threatening in the distance or even over the cube? Was the storm a refreshing and clearing storm? What do you make of it?

Note your interpretations here:

....

....

....

....

....

I hope you found that exercise informative. What did you learn about yourself? What's stayed with you? I hope it showed you that your unconscious is real and, through symbolism and imagination, we have a secret key to access it. These types of exercises help you to see more deeply into your unconscious and to gain some insight into what's really going on. Things in life change, and how we perceive our life changes over time. What we have done here is simply a reflection of how you perceive your life right now. Just reflect on whichever part or parts of this exercise caught your attention.

Dreams

Simply put, dreams are a letter from our unconscious, letting our conscious brain know what it needs to pay attention to.

Dreams are highly interpretative. They are abstract and obscure. If you learn one thing about interpreting dreams in this section, it's that all the objects in dreams represent a part of *you*. If we can keep that one thing in mind, it will help to unravel the messages being sent.

I would like you to keep a dream diary. So many people tell me that they don't remember their dreams, but as soon as you start to pay attention to them you'd be surprised how much more you can recall your dreams. It's like a muscle that needs training – the more you pay attention to your dreams, the more readily you'll be able to access them.

The symbolic nature of dreams is unique to the individual. So if, for example, you keep dreaming about Harry Potter (I had a patient who did) and can't work out the connection, you need to work out what Harry Potter means to *you* – uniquely to you. To do this, try saying the first five words that come into your mind when you think about that particular subject. Don't judge them, just freely associate. It may help you make some connections.

When we worked out what Harry Potter symbolised to my patient and worked through it, she no longer dreamed of Harry Potter. So we knew that we'd resolved something that the unconscious was asking us to pay attention to.

Just as the interpretation of dreams is individual, so are the dreams themselves. But here are a few common dreams that may help you to start thinking in a psychodynamic way. Remember that your personal interpretation and the connections you make are the most important.

Common dreams

Falling

Maybe in your dream you fall out of the sky, off a roof, from a building, through the air or from a car. This may mean that you or your thoughts have gone too high, are too grandiose. Depending on where you land from the fall, a falling dream can also indicate that there is something that is falling into place.

With this in mind, write down what you remember and then apply your interpretation. See which interpretation feels closer to what is or ought to be happening in your life.

Flying

Flying dreams are often similar to falling dreams. Are you flying too high? They can also mean you're on your way to a great overestimation of yourself or your abilities and so ought to be careful.

Naked in front of a big group of people

This may mean you're showing up in reality as a naive person. Or maybe you are showing everything to everyone who comes along without protecting yourself as well as you might. It can also mean that you're embarrassed that you show so much of who you are, or that you feel unprepared in your life at this present moment. Despite this feeling, you may be outwardly projecting an image of invulnerability.

Arriving at school for a big test for which you're unprepared

The core message from this dream is that 'more' is needed from you. You need to prepare yourself more for whatever is going on in your life. You need to anticipate more what might happen, what the trajectory is that you are on and what the potential challenges on that trajectory are.

Phone not working

This dream is related to another type of dream in which you need to make an urgent call or cry for help but whatever you need to do this on is out of order. This dream is common if you find yourself waiting too long to take care of business or to take good care of yourself. The calling for help but getting the wrong number, or the phone being out of order, can also mean that your psyche is trying to correct an imbalance. Your unconscious is calling attention to something in enormous need and is unable to make you consciously listen to what's really going on. So in dreams like this you must ask yourself: where am I not listening to myself? Where have I closed off communication with whatever it is my unconscious is trying to tell me?

Being imprisoned/trapped

The centre of this is that something of great value in your unconscious, a part of you, may feel constrained and frightened. Consider this type of dream as a letter from home: "Look at the condition you're in! Look at what you have done to yourself through the choices you have made or through a twist of fate – you must do something about it!" Dreams give us a clear mirror image of what your situation is psychically in the unconscious. Dreaming of being imprisoned can mean that something is overly contained, without life, not free any longer.

Being chased by a monster or a nearby menacing force (human/weather, etc.)

This dream often means that a great shift is taking/has taken place that means you require additional care, healing or resources in order for the psyche to remain safe and whole.

Losing teeth/hair

We use our teeth not only to grasp things with but to grind things in order to gain their essence (food in particular) or to articulate speech. Teeth carry a broad realm of features and are used symbolically in life for expression, pleasure or communication. When you dream about teeth, ask yourself, "Where am I losing my ability to get nourishment, to give pleasure to others or to myself, or to make myself heard and understood?"

Dreaming about losing hair is a bit different. In old mythology it symbolises quality of ideas/strength and ability in the world. In the Bible, Samson was a creative man who excelled at dominating and leading people. Cutting his hair reduced his strength and power in the world. If you have a dream about losing hair, ask yourself, "How am I losing my ability to generate ideas? How am I thinning out my ideas prematurely? How am I losing my strength to have a creative life?"

Being late and missing a plane/train/bus appointment
This is a familiar anxiety dream: you made a promise to be somewhere and somehow everything goes wrong. In this dream the vehicle represents the attitude you take to go forward in life. If the vehicle you miss is a broken-down taxi, it means your mindset is broken down. If you miss a modern diesel train but the dream takes place in the 1940s, ask yourself: what in the dream is futuristic and out of date at the same time? You may think you're seeing the future but are behind the times.

Animals
In dreams where you see – or feel you are – an animal, we need to look at what the animal represents. A bear has claws and jaws. How does this apply to your life? A horse is considered noble – how does that apply to your life? Fish can dive deep into the darkness and survive under the sea. What is it about a fish and its life that is like something in your life right now?

Animals represent the instinctive nature of your psyche – the part filled with good instincts for loving, living, community life, feeding, hunting, resting and playing. When animals are in your dream and they are whole, it represents a certain wholeness in your psyche. When they are injured in your dreams, there may be an injury to one of the instincts in your psyche that needs to be repaired.

Remember that your personal associations will elaborate the dream greatly over and above the common meanings attributed to animals.

(Interpretations inspired by *The Beginner's Guide to Dream Interpretation* by Clarissa Pinkola Estes.)

Consolidation

It is only by taking a deeper and more holistic approach to unexplained infertility that we may be able to start explaining the unexplainable. Put simply, there may be events in your life that need to be brought from your unconscious into the conscious. In this chapter I have tried to help you to see yourselves not just as parents of wanted-for sons and daughters, but also as sons and daughters of parents. When we understand that stress can be a result of unresolved conflicts or unconscious anxiety, we can do something about it. Through processing and understanding, we can begin to resolve what may feel unresolved, even if we weren't aware of it before we started this chapter. Consequently, we reduce stress or – even better – we unblock. This is the key to your truly authentic mindset and is what makes this approach different to others that try to force an *inauthentic* mindset.

If we can resolve whatever may have caused distress in the past, is causing distress in the present or perhaps even causes fear about the future, it clears a way for the unconscious mind to catch up with the conscious one – the one that wants to become a parent.

Chapter 8

Understanding your Emotions:
Taming the Roller Coaster

How are you feeling? When we're asked that question, what do we all say? Without thought: "Fine, thanks, how are you?" Okay, so let me ask you again. How are you really?

Patients often tell me that they don't really let anyone around them know how they really feel. We all know how isolating this infertility experience can be, but when we do this it can mean that we neglect our emotional well-being. It's completely understandable to hide our feelings – people say stupid things, after all. It may also be that perhaps we don't want to burden other people with our problems. I also see a lot of patients simply wanting to please others and protect them from the crushing nature of the infertility roller coaster. Also, as I've mentioned before, saying things out loud makes them real. So we sometimes avoid saying what may be causing us pain. This tendency to invalidate and suppress our feelings has become part of our culture. For many of us, it's how we've been taught to behave. But one thing is certain – the emotional experience of infertility really is a roller coaster.

In this chapter we are going to flex your emotional intelligence muscles. Recognising your emotions and learning to manage them is one of the most important skills you can have; and I promise you, we are not as good at being emotional as we think.

So what are emotions and why are we thinking about them?

First of all, emotions are subjective. There's nothing worse than someone telling you how you are or how you should be feeling. I cannot change what you've been through, but what I want us to try to do together in this chapter is to find ways of making things a little easier emotionally. When we can, understanding our emotions makes it possible for us to manage them. By managing them, we can make them work for us rather than against us. And when our emotions are working for us, our mindset is inexorably improved. By learning to actively manage your emotions in this chapter, you are taking steps towards becoming more emotionally resilient. This is important, because infertility is hard.

I can imagine it feels like your resilience has already taken a few knocks. I've seen the tendency, within fertility, to adopt a 'keep going until it works' mentality. I understand why this is the attitude of many infertile couples, but I've also seen the burnout and emotional bankruptcy that can be a consequence of this mindset.

The sunk cost theory

Without judgement, there is a tendency, especially among people going through IVF, to approach fertility as something of a relentless process of repeated cycles. It's as though you've gone to Las Vegas and you've decided to bet on red 27. Red 27 doesn't come up, but you've already invested, so you go again. This time when it doesn't work, it hurts a little more than the first. But you go again. Instead of withdrawing, taking it as a loss, processing that loss and moving on, you bet again. You put even more money on red 27. Black 11 comes up – you're bust. Then you think, "I'm in this far, I may as well keep going. Next time it will work." You bet on red 27 again – bust. On and on you go until you have bet everything and you are running on empty.

Like a gambler, you may feel like you have become addicted to the idea of investing until the gamble pays off. It's understandable, of course – ultimately that's what you want: a baby. That's the payout. But the sunk cost theory is that you keep investing in the gamble without processing the emotional fallout of losing – emotionally, relationship-wise, financially... You keep going till either you win (a baby comes along) or you're bust – psychologically, financially and socially. There is also a school of thought which suggests that even after you get the baby this might all catch up with you at some point in the future.

So what's the alternative? We must slow down. But that's really hard – time is not on our side in infertility, after all. That's why I'm not telling you to stop trying. I'm saying let's do it with a different awareness and a different mindset so you don't reach emotional bankruptcy. It's about being reflective and understanding what you've been through, rather than having a compulsion to deal with it by jumping straight back in.

Let's start by putting some emotions into words. No matter how you feel, good or bad, it's a valuable way to start processing and creating an alternative mindset.

So let me ask you again: how are you really? How do you feel? How is your mindset right now?

Emotions by themselves are neither good nor bad. They are simply reactions. However (and this is the important bit), *the way we act (or don't act) on our emotions can strongly affect our well-being.* If you remember, we touched on this before: when we take steps to shut down negative feelings and their associated emotions, we inadvertently shut ourselves down to positive ones too. Sadly, we cannot selectively numb the emotions we want to lose. When we switch off anger and sadness, we switch off happiness and joy too.

We get mixed messages about emotions. When you were younger, you may have been told to "stop crying", "don't come back here until you've sorted yourself out" or "don't be so sensitive". This can start to invalidate how we feel. Can you think of any messages you received as a child? Were you given space to have your feelings? How did your parents (or caregivers) respond when you were upset? Did you feel like you could talk to them when you were angry or when you felt misunderstood?

Many of us have been conditioned to dread negative feelings, and consequently we put a lot of effort into avoiding unpleasant emotions. And our escape routes aren't always that healthy: alcohol, drugs, food and being busy are common examples.

In my experience, the emotional crisis of infertility is extremely difficult to navigate. Emotions serve a helpful role in our lives by motivating us to act quickly in ways that will maximise our chances of survival and success. But when we perceive those emotions as bad, or when some emotional fallout has been too much, our brains work in certain ways to protect us. Often this protection manifests itself as PTSD, which is often present in cases of infertility.

Infertility trauma

As we discussed at the start of the book, going through stressful, frightening or distressing events is sometimes called trauma. When we talk about emotional or psychological trauma, we might mean situations or events we find traumatic and/or how we are affected by our experiences. Traumatic events can happen at any age and can cause long-lasting harm. It's common for women who go through fertility treatments to experience symptoms of PTSD.

It is thought that trauma arises not only because of physical threats to our bodies but also from our emotional and psychological reactions to things that happen – particularly things that we were not expecting. The difficulties you're facing with falling pregnant or maintaining your pregnancy go against how things 'ought to be'. So in much the same way as someone threatening you physically would cause some trauma, so too may your current situation. It's only compounded by your friends and family regularly pressing you for progress reports!

Many people have PTSD from recurrent miscarriages or recurrent IVF failures. All too often a person who has been traumatised by infertility tends to judge themselves or even reject that it's a trauma at all: "I haven't been in a car crash, I haven't been to war. Why would I have anything like PTSD?" However, something as simple as getting your period can set off an episode of PTSD. If you've had a miscarriage and you get your period, that bleeding can trigger PTSD in the form of a panic attack or something similar. There is often a sense of shame about this – that it should be minimised. After all, you're only getting a period! But the mind may recognise this as a flashback of sorts. Bleeding is, on both a conscious and an unconscious level, associated with a trauma. So, much like a soldier associating a ceiling fan with a helicopter and a battlefield, when the mind makes these connections it can cause difficulties.

Symptoms of PTSD can include:
- recurrent nightmares
- suddenly feeling like the trauma is happening right now (flashbacks)
- acute distress accompanying any reminders of the trauma
- feeling pain, unwell, sweating or shaking with no apparent cause
- unexpected images or thoughts coming to mind.

Okay, so now we understand all of this, what do we do with it?

We can understand our emotions better by breaking them down into three components:

1. a subjective component (how you experience the emotion)
2. a physiological component (how your body reacts to the emotion)
3. an expressive component (how you behave in response to the emotion).

Now, I really want to emphasise this point: however you are feeling is okay. Whatever you've gone through, if it was traumatic then it *is* a traumatic experience.

When we bottle up how we are feeling, the emotions don't go away, and when they come back they only come back stronger – with potentially worse consequences. One way to think of this is like putting a lid on a boiling pan. If you've spent a lot of time trying to suppress your feelings, you might find that it feels overwhelming when you do express them.

In the short term, suppressing our feelings might mean overreacting in situations. Maybe you're having an argument with your partner and you explode unexpectedly, or overreact to situations that wouldn't normally bother you. In the long term it can have much more serious consequences, leading to issues such as depression, anxiety and sleep disorders.

With infertility, each consecutive failure or setback on the journey has a cumulative effect on your well-being. It's quite normal, even though pregnancy and a baby are the things that they want the most in the world, for people to create a sort of detachment from it. They are trying to self-protect. "Every time I fail at this, every time I don't achieve pregnancy or having a baby, it hurts me, so I'm going to shut that down. I'm going to shut down those feelings and create a bit of detachment." In reality this doesn't work, because if you have a miscarriage or an unsuccessful treatment it's going to hurt, whether you think you're detached or not.

The importance of your emotions and your mindset

One of the things I've noticed when dealing with infertility is that there seems to be a pressure to be positive when, actually, it's almost impossible to feel positive in the face of adversity. Having a positive mindset is important, but there will be days when you may not even feel like getting out of bed. There may even be days when you are so angry or so heartbroken that you feel consumed by these emotions. You're allowed to feel whatever you're feeling, so give yourself permission to do exactly that. There's no right or wrong – you cannot 'think' yourself into a pregnancy. If you could then you would have done it already.

The key to a healthy mindset is to be realistic about what feels right to you and to understand that mindsets can shift. If you're feeling terrible but you feel like you 'should' have a positive mindset, and so you force yourself to perform that way outwardly, then all you are doing is betraying how you really feel. If your mindset betrays how you really feel, then there is a conflict. I'm not going to encourage you to force a false mindset.

So many approaches do precisely that – they encourage a false mindset. This 'be positive and it'll all be okay' approach is, at best, irritating to those who receive it. At worst, it's damaging to your emotions, your well-being and your mindset. If you're thinking one thing but feeling another, it causes anxiety. I'm not going to betray you by asking you to think that way. Quite the opposite – I'm here to help you. Arguably, if we don't pay attention to emotions that aren't getting the attention they deserve, it will be harder to foster and maintain a positive mindset, as all your energy is going into creating a false one. Your mindset and your emotions are not set in stone. They can change, and they need to be flexible.

To get a realistic, healthy and helpful mindset, we need to get these emotions regulated.

Triggers

We've mentioned before about being careful about how much you expose yourself to social media. Because of the way social media is designed, everyone exposes only a carefully curated version of themselves online. You rarely hear about the difficult periods in someone's life – they just tend to go offline for a while, and then it's back to memes, or holiday and food photos with captions. It's designed to set us up to feel bad about ourselves and to compete to be better – even more so when you're going through all the emotions and upset of infertility. It's not an exaggeration to say it's dangerous.

But what about the benefits of meeting people in the same boat as you online? Initially, infertility-focused social media will bring you to a group of people going through the same thing as you. This can give you a feeling of support. However, the double-edged sword is that when one of these people is successful, this can be something of a trigger for you. Equally, if something goes wrong for another member of the group – if they have a miscarriage or go through an IVF treatment that doesn't work – you end up constantly comparing yourself with them. This is the hidden danger of social media: what may seem like an initially sensible idea can turn sour very quickly. This too will inevitably affect your mindset, so approach social media with caution.

Let's take a moment to think about some of the common emotions that infertility tends to trigger.

Grief and loss

Grief and loss are complex – so complex that I've chosen to dedicate a whole chapter to them (Chapter 9). For the moment, let's just say that they are both typical emotions, but they are not felt in a typical way.

The harsh reality is that you can go through a very costly round of IVF and there is no guarantee it will work. We're used to simple transactions: we pay our money and get what we paid for. Sadly, with IVF this just is not the case. In reality, the success rate of IVF is around 35%. A failure here causes feelings of grief and loss, and there are no refunds.

Isolation

Infertility has a cumulative effect. Hearing news of other pregnancies or births can mean that you don't want to be around other people's success so much because you don't want to seem grumpy or jealous. You may have had to take a break from your career because you're going through an assisted reproduction intervention. Again, more isolation. Infertility takes over everything. Your life is consumed by a constant infertility cycle, so getting your period can be really upsetting, but this isn't something you feel you can share with others. Then you're waiting and waiting – alone – until you ovulate again.

Anger

Anger is one of the most powerful and misunderstood emotions. Unfortunately, our judgements around anger – or, more likely, our fear around being angry – can lead to anger suppression. But did you know that anger can be healthy? When it's expressed in a healthy way, anger is not a negative emotion. At the end of the day, it's completely normal for you to feel anger (among all the other emotions) when you realise you're not pregnant or that something has gone wrong.

When we judge our anger it can quickly turn into guilt or shame. So we try to bury feelings of anger. But remember: anger is not aggression. They are not the same thing. Anger is healthy whereas aggression is not. Suppressed anger has been linked to a variety of physical and mental health issues from hypertension to depression. Take a look at the conversation below:

> **Louise:** *Elena, you seem very agitated. Can I ask what's going on?*
> **Elena:** *I'm fine. I'm just a bit tired today. I don't know what's going on with me. Well, something is going on, but it's really nothing.*
> **Louise:** *I'd like to hear about it, whatever it is.*
> **Elena:** *I'm so fucking…gosh, sorry, didn't mean to swear.*
> **Louise:** *It's fine, I don't mind at all. You're so fucking…?*
> **Elena:** *Angry!*
> **Louise:** *Okay, there we go! What's happened?*
> **Elena:** *It's really nothing, what…er… Perhaps we could think about something else.*

Louise: *We can think about whatever you would like, but I'd like to understand what is going on, if you'd like to tell me?*

Elena: *I would like to…*

Louise: *But?*

Elena: *I'm worried you'll judge me.*

Louise: *For?*

Elena: *For being angry.*

Louise: *Why would I judge you?*

Elena: *It's just so ugly.*

Louise: *What makes you say that?*

Elena: *(silent sighing)*

Louise: *Does it feel like I'm judging you?*

Elena: *No.*

Louise: *Good – I'm not. I'm trying to understand you and perhaps let you know that it's okay to be angry. I am here for you, however you may be feeling.*

It's okay to be angry. But the key here, again, is to start naming these feelings and not view anger as a negative emotion. Anger can sometimes work as a defence mechanism. When we get into fight-flight-freeze mode, fight can look a bit like anger. So you might start taking it out on your partner or they may take it out on you. The source of the anger may be the fertility clinic or your family or anyone around you, but if we suppress anger, that's when it tends to accumulate and explode.

Anxiety and foreboding

Who wouldn't be anxious about going through all of this? It's hard to keep positive and hopeful when the historical evidence shows us that all may not work out well. As we tend to go with the evidence rather than blindly remaining hopeful at all times, it's understandable that the future looks ominous. So what can you do if you have feelings like this? I often find that taking a break from social media is helpful. I've also found that my patients can find some relief by simply connecting with and being with others – whether they are people going through the same thing or are completely unconnected with the infertility you're experiencing.

Shame, blame and guilt

Shame and guilt are very closely connected but – and we've mentioned this before – shame and blame are also good bedfellows. In MUI, where there isn't a reason for your infertility, the conclusion that many women I work with come to is that the fault lies with them. This makes them feel shameful. When they see others around them who are not 'failing' – who have families – it can become a shameful and isolating experience.

Guilt is feeling that you've done something wrong; shame is feeling that you *are* something wrong. Through the work we're doing in this chapter, I want to help you develop a more compassionate internal voice. If someone you know were going through what you're going through, there is no way you'd say to them the things you are secretly saying to yourself. Through the coming exercises, we will help to develop that kinder internal voice.

Well-being

Recognising and understanding your emotions is vital for your well-being, but we are not as good at it as we think we are! Emotions are our body's way of communicating with us about what is going on. Of course some feelings are more difficult than others, but they are equally important, and what matters is how you react to your feelings and acknowledge them as they arise. An important part of knowing your emotional experience is understanding which part of your body is activated by a particular emotion. The more connected you are with yourself and the more you understand your emotional responses, the easier it is to deal with life's challenges. And you are being challenged right now.

Being true to yourself

We're going to work on giving you a true sense of how you're feeling, because that will neutralise a lot of anxiety. It's okay to hate going to the fertility clinic and have your bloods taken every morning. You're allowed to say this. What's more, you need to create a space where you're *allowed* to say it. You don't have to say to yourself, "I'll get through it, I can cope with this, I can do this."

This is a little like coaching yourself. Yes, that's right – your **inner** therapist can work as a coach as well! Infertility is a minefield of hundreds of different emotions that you can feel in a short period of time. I'm not saying I know all the emotions. Without being with you in person, I can't tell you all the emotions you're feeling right now. But in my experience there are certain 'flavours' of emotions that go with infertility. I'm going to give you some exercises around these emotions so that you can tailor your own approach to your infertility.

Exercise 1: Identifying your emotional state

I'd like us to get a current baseline for your emotional state.

Ask yourself: how well do I feel right now?

Now I'd like you to have a go at the following feelings chart. I'm yet to have a patient where doing this has not proved helpful, as it identifies the nuances of how you may be feeling.

Note five emotions that match your current emotional state here.

1. ....
....

2. ....
....

3. ....
....

4. ....
....

5. ....
....

Okay, we've established your current emotional baseline. Now I'm going to ask you to review the letter you wrote to your pregnant self in Chapter 3.

How do you feel now? Can you remember when you wrote the letter? How did it make you feel at the time? Reviewing it today, how does it make you feel now? How does it make you feel that I'm asking you to do it again? How does your body feel? Do you notice any sensations?

Now note down the five active emotions that match your emotional state right here in this moment.

1. ....

....

2. ....

....

3. ....

....

4. ....

....

5. ....

....

Let's keep going. What emotions have come up for you using this workbook so far? I'm going to challenge you! Be true to how you really feel, even if the emotion you have about the workbook is "This workbook is starting to get on my nerves – where is the magic formula? Why do I have to do all this work?" Or are you starting to feel understood? Are you starting to feel heard? The important point here is that you don't deny how you *really* feel, because when you name how you feel this means that your mind, body and emotions are all working in concert. This is how you create an authentic mindset.

How do you feel?

1. ....

....

2. ....

....

3. ....

....

4. ....

....

5. ....

....

Exercise 2: The five senses

Now I'd like to ground you in your emotional state using a technique known as 'the five senses'. It's a helpful exercise to do if you are feeling overwhelmed or anxious. You just need to just take a minute to ground yourself – I'm going to show you how.

First, find a place that's quiet. If that's not possible then find a way to quiet your mind, and close your eyes and breathe deeply. Let's give this a try. We're going to count down from five.

5: Look around the room and see if you can notice five things that you ordinarily wouldn't pay attention to. Not big things like a TV or a light, but things like a small crack, a shadow or maybe a mark on a window.

4: Moving on to your hearing, focus on four things you can hear. Can you hear birds outside? Maybe you can hear someone working outside, a lawnmower, a sprinkler or an aeroplane. Just notice, that's all I want you to do.

3: Now I want you to notice three things that you can feel. They could be things like what your feet can feel – for example, are you barefoot on a rug? How does it feel between your toes? What do your clothes feel like against your skin? What are your hands resting on?

2: How about two things that you can smell? Really open your nostrils (flare them if you can – I can't). Do you smell anything nice? Or maybe something not so nice. I want you to pay attention and notice.

1: Lastly, what can you taste? Nothing? Have a sip of a drink – it's allowed.

The point of this simple exercise is to increase your mindfulness by giving your brain something to do in the present moment. Cliched as it is, to 'take a moment to stop and smell the flowers' is something we ought to do more. Try to remember how this exercise makes you feel, and be willing to use it any time you feel a little overwhelmed. Also, notice which of the senses resonated with you the most and held your attention. I find it helps me to become grounded when my mind is racing.

If you're feeling anxious, now is a good time to ask yourself: *in this present moment*, what's wrong? Do you have any problems *in this moment?* When I ask this question it's not uncommon to hear my patients say something like, "I can't think about that at the moment – there's just too much going on." I understand. You can use this senses exercise to calm the maelstrom in your mind, to hit the brakes and come back to the here and now. It's hard to access, but this is a great way of breaking the vicious cycle of anxiety.

I know a lot of women who use this exercise when going through a fertility treatment, for example if they're going to do a transfer or have eggs collected, or if they're waiting for news about something. They find that they're anticipating what the news is going to be, but the reality is that you can't control what the news is going to be. What you *can* do is help yourself to feel a little more centred.

Exercise 3: Breathing: 4–7–8

We all have an inbuilt machine in our bodies to help us calm down. When we feel anxious or are anticipating the future, our sympathetic nervous system is activated. This is what makes us slip into the fight-flight-freeze mode. But we also have a parasympathetic nervous system, which acts to calm us down and balance out the activated part of ourselves. The way to activate this system is through breathing.

I see people all the time who do not breathe (properly). We all know how to breathe – we're all sitting here talking, reading and breathing. We just don't breathe properly. For most of us, this means that we tend to take very shallow breaths. The following technique helps you to breathe deeply and activate your parasympathetic nervous system to let your body rest and digest. It slows the heart rate and also serves to bring you into the present. Again, it gives your brain something to do. You're thinking about breathing and nothing else. Close your mouth and inhale quietly through your nose to a mental count of four.

- Hold your breath for a count of seven.
- Slowly exhale completely through your mouth with your lips pursed so you can hear the air leaving you to a count of eight.
- Now inhale again and repeat the cycle three more times for a total of four breaths.

What do you notice?

....

....

....

....

....

....

....

....

....

Exercise 4: Compassion

This is where we're going to counteract the voice in your head that tells you that you are doing a bad job or that you are a failure. We're not going to be able to get rid of the critical voice straight away – we can't just say "I've decided to be kind to myself, so it will happen". You've probably had years and years of a very loud voice. It may be that, right now, the volume of your internal critic is turned up all the way to eleven. What we can do is counteract your internal critic with a compassionate, non-judgemental voice – the kind voice of your inner fertility therapist. This will mean that, once again, your mind is working in balance – the sympathetic nervous system and the parasympathetic nervous system working together – the bully and the soother.

I want you to write down some of the typical mean things that you catch yourself saying internally on a day-to-day basis. Be honest.

Write here.

....

....

....

....

....

What's it like to read that back? Maybe you could even try saying them out loud. It doesn't feel very good, does it?

Now, can you counteract each one with how you would respond to a friend or someone else close to you who was voicing that same narrative?

Write here.

....

....

....

....

....

Exercise 5: Conscious compassion

To try this exercise, sit somewhere quiet where you won't be disturbed, and begin to focus on your breathing. Think about a time when you felt very kind and caring towards a person or a beloved animal.

Try not to choose a time when that person or animal was distressed, because then you are likely to focus on that distress instead of the kind, compassionate feelings for them.

Next, focus on the desire you felt to help the person or animal, and the feelings of kindness that guided you to help. Remember that in this exercise it is your intentions that are important, not how the person or animal responds.

As you bring to mind a specific time when you felt compassionate towards them, imagine yourself expanding, as if you are becoming calmer, wiser, stronger, more responsible and better able to help them.

Pay attention to your body as you remember how it felt to be kind. Spend some time expanding with warmth in your body. Notice the genuine desire for this person to be free from suffering and to flourish.

Spend a minute or two thinking about the tone of your voice and the kinds of things you said, or the kinds of things you did or wanted to do to help.

Spend another minute or two thinking about how good it felt to be kind to them.

Finally, focus only on your desire to be helpful and kind: the sense of warmth, feelings of expansion, your kind tone of voice, the wisdom in your voice and your behaviour.

When you have finished this exercise, you may want to take some notes about how this felt for you.

....

....

....

....

....

....

....

Building your resilience

Resilience is how we adapt when things don't go to plan. In our case this is fertility, but it can be anything – any other tragedy, trauma, threat or stressful event (family, work, money, etc.). Perhaps you have found that infertility has diminished your sense of resilience.

What can you do if you don't feel resilient?

Learning to be kinder to yourself in general can help you control the amount of pressure you feel in different situations, which can help you feel less stressed. Are you seeing the pattern here? Kindness is key.

You should make the time to recognise and reward your achievements, no matter how small. You could maybe take a walk, read a book, treat yourself to food you enjoy, or simply tell yourself "Well done". Even spending a day in a different place can help you feel more able to face stress and the all-consuming nature of infertility.

Forgive yourself when you feel you have made a mistake or when you don't achieve something you hoped for. Try to remember that nobody's perfect and that putting extra pressure on yourself doesn't help.

Managing uncertainty

We're hardwired to always be second guessing what will happen next. It's where déjà vu comes from (sometimes our mind correctly anticipates what's about to happen). When it comes to fertility, there are two main sources of uncertainty. The first is simply why you're unable to conceive or maintain your pregnancy. Is my period going to come? Is there something wrong with me or us? The medical community are scratching their heads too – there's nothing medically wrong, so what gives? Secondly, even if the medical community agrees to go down a route of one intervention or another (IVF, etc.), there's no guarantee that it will be successful. More uncertainty. It's not hard to see why what you're going through is hitting the uncertainty button.

If we increase your understanding that uncertainly is inevitable then we can, once again, reduce anxiety. As we now know, less anxiety means less stress, and less stress increases the chances of pregnancy. What follows are a few techniques which I have found can help to reduce uncertainty-induced anxiety and tame your emotional roller coaster.

Techniques for coping with uncertainty

- **Identify (and tune out) unproductive worrying.** Again, this is about noticing. First, to tune out, you have to notice and tune in. So what's going on in my head? This feels quite punitive. It feels like I'm not speaking to myself very nicely or that my worry is out of control. Identify it and then use habits and routines to get a sense of control. If things feel out of control to you right now, what can you do that you *can* control? Consider the exercise we did before around things you can control and things you cannot control.
- **Seek out humour.** Humour is a defence, but it's a very healthy defence. Try to remember something that you've laughed about or found funny. It doesn't have to be comically wonderful – it's just something to help break the tension.
- **Don't rely on temporary distractions.** Distractions are good, but we need the distractions to be healthy. So if you are scrolling through social media, what you're most likely doing is seeking comfort and soothing. In reality, while it may initially help, social media works to keep your worry or anxiety more pervasive. So use the techniques from this workbook instead.
- **Practice mindfulness** (our 5–4–3–2–1, compassion and 4–7–8 exercises).
- **Accept what you can't control by focusing on what you can control.**

Exercise 6: What else can I do?

Another area I have found to be helpful when working with my infertility patients is Acceptance and Commitment Therapy. This is an approach which considers your behaviour and what we can do to increase your psychological resilience. We achieve this by, once again, leveraging mindfulness techniques as well as introducing some diffusion techniques. This means interrupting the unhelpful emotions and disrupting their presence and subsequent power.

Here are a few things you can try when your emotions are getting the better of you.

Thanks, Brain: Next time your mind starts sending you on a downward spiral – stop. Acknowledge what your mind is doing with a simple "Thank you, brain". Your mind 'thinks' it's helping you but you've consciously noticed that it isn't.

Close that Pop-Up: We know how frustrating Internet pop-up ads can be. When your mind pings something unhelpful into your thoughts, imagine you're seeing a pop-up advert and just click on the 'Close (X)' button. Not today, brain – no thanks.

Saaaaaay it Sloooowly: Has an unpleasant thought come into focus? Say the thought in your mind repeatedly, but each time say it more slowly than the last. Keep going until it's reeeeaaally slow. By doing this, almost in a comically slow voice in your mind, you can take the negative power away from the thought.

Driftwood: Negative thought? Place it on a piece of driftwood, push it out into a river and watch it float away. Powerfully simple.

Narrator: If you hear yourself saying "I just know this is going to fail", change the voice to that of your favourite actor (such as Morgan Freeman) and change it to "Louise had the thought that she was going to fail". Again, surprisingly effective.

As with all these techniques, they're not 'one and done'. You need to keep trying them. If you like, take this page out of the workbook and keep it with you.

Now let's consolidate these techniques with my favourite (and arguably the most effective) tool: gratitude.

Exercise 7: Gratitude

This is one of my favourite practices because it's instant first aid, an instant hug. In fact, practising gratitude before you go to bed has been shown to be one of the most effective ways of helping you sleep. Gratitude unshackles us from toxic emotions and has lasting effects on the brain.

Three ways to practise gratitude

- The smartest way of doing this is simply to think about five things that you are grateful for. Gratitude is an incredibly powerful tool. It doesn't have to be anything massive. You could be grateful for a nice coffee, that the sun is out or that it's raining and you don't have to go out. It's the simple things that can change your frame of mind from negative into positive.
- Savour, absorb and really pay attention to the good things.
- Express your gratitude to yourself, write it down or thank someone.

Sexercise

Perhaps sex has become all about fertility and as a result has become more of a 'chore' than about intimacy and connection. The act of lovemaking releases a feel-good chemical in your brain called oxytocin. Some people think that oxytocin helps with fertility. It's the same chemical that is released in your brain during childbirth and lactation.

I had a patient going through fertility treatment who hadn't had an orgasm for six (very long) years. Her homework was to go home and have an orgasm. She wasn't big into 'self-care' but I insisted (in a very kind way) that she needed that release, so off she went. She returned the following week and told me that the way she felt in her body afterwards was completely different – that her orgasm released a lot of tension. This was a point of great healing for her.

Sex, orgasms and oxytocin are all natural and good for us. Our bodies and mind need to have that release of tension, otherwise you will just hold onto it. I'm not saying that furious masturbation will make you pregnant, but it can't hurt! Try also to have sex for the sake of sex – not just to make a baby. After all, you are more than just a baby-making machine.

Consolidation

It's easy to believe the fallacy that you must always be in (and maintain) a positive mindset. While I'm not denying that mindset is important, it must be an authentic, realistic and healthy one. To get to this mindset we must find a way of containing, regulating and processing the emotional part of you. If we don't do this, there is conflict. Your mind is saying "I must be positive it's going to happen this time; it's going to work", whereas your real emotions are saying "I hate this so much, this is never going to work, I'm such a failure".

A healthy and realistic mindset might look something like "This has been really hard, I'm hurting right now, but I'm trying the best I can". It's not denial and it's not the doom and gloom of "This will never work, I'll always be a failure" – it's simply "I'm doing the best I can."

You are doing the best you can. I know that you are. Remind yourself of this as many times as you need to.

I hope you've found that the exercises and the experience of working through this chapter have helped you get to that healthy mindset. I also hope this chapter has given you the ability to put yourself into a mindset that's realistic. After all, a healthy mindset is one where your mind and your emotions are aligned.

So let me ask you again: how are you feeling? Really?

Chapter 9

Your Relationship with Loss: Grieving the Child that Wasn't

Here we are then, at our final session together. In a therapeutic setting, this would be the natural conclusion of our sessions. The ending of our time together is, in its own way, a loss. When you feel ready, I would like us to work through this chapter together.

Sadly, this chapter doesn't offer a fix or a cure to the devastating effects of loss. I'm not going to tell you that I can make it better, but what I can tell you is that working through your losses sensitively and compassionately will help you towards a place of grieving, healing and clearing.

When we experience loss, we tend to feel a huge range of emotions – sometimes all at the same time, which can be overwhelming. Grief is an intensely powerful emotion and can be a physical reaction to the loss of someone or something. You may have deep feelings of sadness or despair and often a powerful longing to be with the person who is missing. This is even more complicated when, in many cases, you haven't met your baby yet. Or you might feel numb and empty, as if there is no point any more. Perhaps you've felt annoyed at yourself for feeling this way instead of how you've been led to believe you 'should' be feeling. Perhaps you feel that you should be coping better.

All this is to say that it's quite normal to experience a range of emotions. One of the most common experiences I see related to loss is the fear that you will never feel better.

Grief can be felt physically, sometimes in waves; not being able to eat or sleep or feeling sick are all normal during grieving. But despite the pain, the process of grieving is an important part of how we come to terms with loss.

Trigger warning

This chapter needs to be undertaken in a safe space. I'd like you to take a moment to work out what a safe space may look like for you – you will need to feel able to be vulnerable. Consider if you are going to work through this chapter alone or with somebody. Is there a way to make sure you can protect some uninterrupted time to do this? I am going to try to hold the pain and the grief with you as much I can, but I need you to take care of your environment and who you have around you.

When I deal with loss in a therapeutic context, I go very gently with it, so I want us to approach this in the same way. If it feels like it's too much, take a step back, take a pause – please trust yourself enough to go at your own pace. If you feel like you want to stop, then stop. If it feels like you aren't ready, then wait until you are. And when you are ready, I hope that this chapter supports you in discovering that grief can be healing.

Loss is tremendously difficult to deal with, and grief and mourning are our natural responses to it. When I work with those who have suffered loss I see that, when the time is right and they finally feel able to acknowledge the loss as real, we're able to reduce their suffering and tension when they feel they are able to grieve.

What we're aiming to achieve together here is for you to be able to accept your losses, grieve for them, and let go of them. Sometimes the fear of feeling the loss is worse than actually feeling it. The pain of grief also brings relief, but most of us fear pain, so we do our best to avoid it altogether.

First steps with loss

Let's start by taking stock of your own relationship to loss. Who have you lost who was important to you? Can you remember what that felt like? Do you feel as though you have grieved for that person?

....

....

....

....

....

....

....

....

....

....

As we work through the exercises in this chapter, it may be worthwhile approaching them in the light of previous losses you have experienced. This workbook is about you as a whole person and all that you've been through to date. Loss is unavoidable, whether it takes the form of a death, losing a job, the end of a relationship, losing hopes and dreams, or losing other things that you value. You have, I hope, developed some tools over the course of this book, so let's put them into practice by naming emotions, reflecting on how they make you feel – especially in the body – and writing them down, talking about them and reflecting on them. And let's do that with the most important caveat that you should be gentle with yourself.

When we think about infertility, there will have been, for some, losses along the way that don't get the attention they need. Maybe some of these scenarios will apply to you, or perhaps some won't – and won't ever. Let's have a think about some of those losses.

Infertility and secondary losses

When we experience loss, we focus on the tangible 'things' that we lose: the person, the house, the job, the relationship, etc. That is, of course, a huge part of grief. But there is this other part of grief that we are often less aware of: the secondary losses that we might brush off but that can create far more to cope with.

Loss of the normal, the easy, the ideal

Your fertility journey likely started out full of hope and anticipation, and it is quite rare that people anticipate the struggles they have subsequently encountered. This means there is a loss of an exciting new chapter, a loss of the celebration around pregnancy and sharing in the good news, as it may feel as though it's too fragile to risk just in case something goes wrong. There can be the loss of the positivity, joy and celebratory nature of pregnancy and starting a family, as it becomes laden with anxiety, anticipation, fear, guilt, shame or anger.

Loss of self and identity

Our identity is the way we think about ourselves, how we define ourselves, the story we tell ourselves about who we are. And yet we don't always have a conscious awareness of our identity until something changes. I wonder what this means to you.

Loss of feeling well, feeling attractive, feeling physically robust

Men with diagnosed male factor issues often report feeling like 'less of a man', because virility is so closely associated with masculinity in our culture. Women tend to struggle with feelings of inadequacy too, or a sense of not being a 'true woman', because fertility and womanhood have traditionally been so strongly linked. This feels like a loss of being connected with the social norms of our society. Perhaps fertility treatments have taken their toll on your body and you're feeling less attractive than you did in the past. These are all real losses.

Loss of self-esteem

Being unable to have a child challenges – and may begin to erode – your self-esteem. This problem can be significantly worse if you have been highly successful in other areas of your life but may not have developed the coping skills to deal with failure and loss.

Loss of relationship and intimacy

For involuntarily childless couples, your whole world can become about infertility and you can become consumed by uncertainty. There is also a loss of spontaneity, as sex becomes only about baby-making. Sex for the sake of pleasure, intimacy and connection is hijacked by infertility and obligation.

Loss of control of the personal body, loss of privacy

I often hear from women who tell me that their bodies feel medicalised and brutalised, that they no longer feel a sense of what it's like to be in their own bodies, as if their bodies have been handed over to medicine. In much the same way, men are asked to produce sperm samples on demand with very little privacy. There is a loss of dignity.

If fertility treatment is part of the picture, there may also be a sense of loss in terms of conception not being the private, personal, intimate and non-medicalised event you had hoped for.

Loss of career, loss of sense of purpose

The impact of infertility on a woman's career is often overlooked, but it shouldn't be underestimated. The challenges of combining fertility treatment and work are stressful – fertility treatment can start to feel like another full-time job.

Perhaps you are concerned about your job security. As women are often the primary focus of the evaluation or treatment, they often have to miss considerable amounts of work. This may place their job in jeopardy. In addition, they often fear telling their employer the reason for their absences, because the employer might assume the treatment will be successful and the woman will therefore be leaving her job. This might put her at risk of being laid off or dismissed.

Loss of friendships and social connections

It can become difficult to celebrate, enjoy and actively participate in the pregnancies and parenthood journeys of close friends and family members. You might feel you've lost the person who used to be happy to share in good news and who would feel excited about attending celebrations and traditions. This might lead to the loss of social connections.

Loss of control

If you are trying to get pregnant – either naturally or through medical intervention – everything can feel controlled while being out of control. Restricted diets, no alcohol, no gluten, not being able to plan as everything is always on hold – it can feel as if you don't have a handle on your own life.

That is a lot of loss.

Loss is hard to deal with; as humans we're not good at it. I wonder if this is because (certainly for the British) we're too 'stiff upper lip' about it – we feel that we mustn't show our emotions. In fertility, loss is particularly hard because it is often not a tangible baby you have lost but the wish/dream/hope for a baby. We are gradually learning to talk about baby loss, and recently there has been more discussion about it on social media, with celebrities talking more openly about miscarriage and its devastating effects. But there is still little open discussion about how you feel when you've lost something you didn't have.

Miscarriage – at any stage in pregnancy – and stillbirth are traumatic experiences. So is the failure of IVF – going through so much to get pregnant and then finding there is something wrong with the baby, or being told that IVF won't work and you'll have to consider surrogacy or egg donation instead; these are all losses.

You may have been in denial about your own losses in any of these areas because they don't seem significant enough, or you may not have been able to grieve. Your brain might even have shut down a little, especially if there is PTSD. It's important to keep in mind that your loss is a trauma, and during therapy we must make all efforts not to retraumatise you. This is because your brain might remember your loss as though it is happening again. That's okay – I will remind you that this is a memory, this is in the past. Remember our earlier exercise about telling and retelling the story of your trauma? It's hard to do, so you must keep yourself in a safe space.

Sometimes it helps to map out your loss. Maybe you started with the loss of the idea that you would fall pregnant naturally, then you moved on to IVF, then you had the loss of the hope that it would happen with IVF, and maybe there were miscarriages. Each leg of the journey represents losses for you. And if none of it has worked, that is the ultimate loss.

With the loss of miscarriage, there is also the public reaction to it. Some of the worst things people say in relation to miscarriages are:

- "At least it was early"
- "At least you know you can get pregnant"
- "At least you didn't even know"
- "At least you're still young"
- "At least you've got lots of time".

These 'at least' phrases all dismiss the loss. The intention is to make you feel better – it's not coming from a bad place. It's just not validating your experience. A well-intentioned comment is still an upsetting comment. If your leg was broken in an accident, no matter how you did it, it would still be a broken leg and people would sympathise. But a broken leg is so much more accessible for others to support you with, because people can see you have a broken leg. They can't see your broken heart.

Miscarriage is so common. If we consider the statistics in the UK:

- an estimated 1 in 4 pregnancies ends in miscarriage
- around 11 in 1,000 pregnancies are ectopic
- about 1 in 100 women in the UK experience recurrent miscarriages (3 or more in a row)
- 29% of women who've experienced miscarriage suffer with PTSD.

And yet, if you have lost a baby in this way, you will know how isolating it can feel. But even in these feelings, you are not alone.

The most common refrains I hear from my patients while we work through this trauma are:

- "I feel broken"
- "I feel unfixable"
- "I feel without purpose"
- "I feel unworthy"
- "I feel unable to refer to myself as a woman"
- "I feel guilty for grieving"

You are none of these.

Loss in secondary infertility is even more overlooked. People say, "At least you already have a baby."

Check in with yourself here. How are you feeling about the losses you have experienced? Remember to treat yourself with sensitivity and compassion.

Once we identify what losses have occurred, we can start to work through them, which brings us to grief. Here is how I help my patients to understand what to expect when grieving. As we know, understanding can help to demystify feelings, so when we know what to expect, we are more likely to go towards rather than away from grief.

The five stages of grief

When we experience loss, the pain can feel overwhelming. It's important to understand that grief is complicated, and we are individuals who have our own unique, emotional expression.

Psychiatrist Elisabeth Kübler-Ross developed a way of understanding how we experience grief – a theory of grieving – that incorporates five distinct stages: denial, anger, bargaining, depression, and finally acceptance.

As we consider these stages, remember that people grieve differently. You may or may not go through all these stages, and you might not go through them in the 'right' order. In fact, the lines of these stages are often blurred – we may move from one to the other and possibly back again before fully moving into a new stage.

There is also no specific time period suggested for any of these stages. Someone may experience the stages quickly, maybe in a matter of weeks, whereas another person may take months or even years to move to a place of acceptance. However long it takes for you to move through them is perfectly normal.

So let's talk about each of them together. I suggest that as we go along, you write down a time when you may have felt like you were in one of the stages.

Denial

Denial is said to be the first stage of grief. It helps us to cope with the overwhelming pain of loss, possibly until we feel we are ready to do so. In the very early stages this can also feel a lot like disbelief. You might not believe that this loss has occurred, or it could feel surreal or disconnected. What we are trying to do here is survive emotional pain.

In this moment of loss it might feel as though our reality has shifted. Sometimes it takes a while for our minds to catch up with what has happened and to adjust to this new reality.

There can be a lot of information to download and a lot of painful imagery to process, and denial attempts to slow this process down and take us through it one step at a time. Its function at this time is to protect us rather than risk feeling overwhelmed by our emotions.

It's important to remember that denial is not an attempt to pretend that the loss does not exist. We are simply trying to delay having to absorb and understand what is happening until it feels safe to do so.

Anger

Remember what we have said in the past about anger? We tend to view it as a negative emotion, but it isn't. In the stages of grieving, anger can help us with emotional processing as it works as something of an outlet. When we experience loss we experience extreme emotional discomfort, and our instinct is to push that away. The anger functions as a defence – it can serve to push people away from us, but it can also serve to push painful emotions away from us.

Anger is often the first thing we feel when we start to release emotions related to loss. This may leave us feeling isolated when actually we could benefit from comfort and connection.

Bargaining

Because infertility necessarily means grieving the loss of an effortless pregnancy, we often see couples begin a bargaining process whereby they attempt to do 'everything right' to get pregnant. They believe that if they work hard enough to get pregnant and do all the right things, they will. They feel helpless, so in an attempt to regain control they 'bargain' through a series of hypothetical statements, such as 'if only' or 'what if'. Bargaining is often accompanied by guilt, and you start to believe that there might have been something you could have done differently. You might even try to make a secret deal with God or some other 'higher power'.

When dealing with the pain of loss, it isn't unusual to feel so desperate that you're willing to do almost anything to alleviate the pain. We can become very aware of our humanness in these moments when we realise there is nothing we can do to influence results.

When we experience loss, it's common to blame ourselves for something we might have done in the past. We wish we could go back and behave differently. We also tend to make the assumption that if things had played out differently, we would not be in such an emotionally painful place in our lives now. This leads to shame, sadness and depression – or even a diversion back to anger.

Depression

During this stage, your guilt or shame may begin to turn into sadness and depression. Your imagination calms down and you slowly start to look at the reality of your situation. You realise that bargaining isn't an option and you are suddenly faced with reality.

This is possibly the hardest stage of the grieving process, but it is key, because it's when you start to develop an understanding of the loss and the effect it's had on your life. The way to navigate this stage is firstly to acknowledge that you are going through a tough time. Maybe we could take a moment to acknowledge that together now?

You see, others around you may try to help you get 'out' of this depression. However, this is not a bad place to be. It's no fun, for sure, but it's not what we may call a clinical depression – it's a natural response to a loss and needs to be experienced in order to heal.

So try not to ignore your emotions. If you feel ready, allow yourself to experience these powerful feelings. In this way we can start to move, slowly and carefully, towards healing. Perhaps it's a good idea to remember this as we start to work through the exercises that follow.

Acceptance

There might be a misconception that if we work though these steps, the pain of infertility will go away. The reality is that, while it may not be deleted from your mind, we can move to a place where it feels more bearable. It is the experience of the emotions and allowing yourself to feel the depression of loss that lead to the stage of acceptance. In other words, sometimes we must go through the pain to come out on the other side of it. It is as though accepting the reality of the losses of infertility creates a space for you to be able to move forwards.

When we come to a place of acceptance, it is not that we no longer feel the pain of loss. Rather, we are no longer *resisting* the reality of our situation or struggling to make it something different. When we stop resisting, we stop creating anxiety and stress. And we allow our mindset to be authentic and realistic.

Remember that sadness and regret can still be present in this phase, but the emotional survival tactics of denial, bargaining and anger are less likely to be present.

We're going to move onto some techniques now, but before we do I want you to think about whether you feel ready, because these exercises are deliberately emotionally provoking.

Marking your own stages of grief

I want us to consider the stages of grief and where you may be in them. This means I am going to challenge you to feel all the feelings. You have the tools to do this now, as this is what we have been working towards. I want us to go through the depression, go through the sadness and move towards the space that is acceptance – that is, letting go. This is where you allow the past to stay in the past and allow yourself to feel more present and resilient, making the future feel less anxious and more hopeful.

Remember: you will need to deploy your most kind and compassionate voice as you work through these with yourself. You will also need the time and space to be able to work through them quietly and mindfully.

Do these exercises when you feel ready. If you were in my office now, we would work out when you felt ready, but I am empowering you to make the call. If you start these exercises and it feels too much, either stop and revisit this another time or get some additional support. Again, you make the call.

You can also choose whether you work through these on your own or with someone. Some patients can't do these exercises collaboratively – at least, not initially. They may go away and do them alone first and then, once they've done them, come back and go through them with a partner. It's your call – go with whatever feels right. If you're ready, let's try the first exercise.

Exercise 1: Timeline

I would like you to map out a timeline of the losses you have experienced. Again, this is about empowering you to make this task your own. I'd like you to focus not only on the fertility losses – the loss of conceiving naturally, the loss of a child, moving to surrogacy or egg donation and losing the chance for the baby to be biologically yours or your partner's

– but also the losses you have suffered over your own lifetime. Have you grieved them? I wonder if there is some special attention that needs to be paid to the death of a loved one in your past that you may still be carrying.

I'd like you to draw a line from left to right and start signposting all the difficult events in your life that have been troubling you recently.

When you've done that, try to do this over your lifespan by adding all the other significant or memorable events during that time.

What we are doing here is, in a way, laying things to rest. There is a lot to be said for pinning things to the earth so they don't follow us around.

Exercise 2: Saying goodbye

Sometimes, where patients have experienced either a miscarriage, a stillbirth or even a health-related termination, I ask them to write it down. I ask them to write a letter to their baby. I knew a couple who did this, and it really helped them. They wrote their letter and then went to the beach and put it in the sea and said goodbye.

Goodbye letter

To ....

I am saying goodbye because

....

....

....

Saying goodbye makes me feel

....

....

....

Something I want you to know

....

....

....

I will always remember

....

....

....

....

From ....

If you have not already taken a break, maybe now is a good time to do so.

Exercise 3: Miscarriage

If you have suffered miscarriage/s, I am truly sorry. The loss associated with miscarriage is underestimated and is not just 'one of those things'.

It is rare for miscarriage not to have trauma attached to it. One of the ways in which we deal with trauma in therapy is to tell the story. You see, the more we expose ourselves to traumatic memories, the more their potency starts to diminish. It's normal to feel uncomfortable when discussing trauma, but you can reassure yourself, when you need to, that the story you are describing is in the past. If it feels too bad, you can always stop.

If it feels okay, I'd like you to take some time to write down your story here. Start with what was happening just before it happened, then go on to what led up to the miscarriage and everything that took place from there onwards.

....

....

....

....

....

....

....

....

....

If you have experienced miscarriage, I urge you to complete the next two exercises. If you have not, then please feel free to skip them.

Exercise 4: Speaking to your baby

Now, this next bit is hard. In fact, when we do this in therapy, it evokes many as yet untouched feelings, so before you do this exercise, check your environment and check in with how you feel.

I am going to ask you: if you had the opportunity to speak to the baby or babies that you lost, what might you say to them?

I need you to speak this aloud. The act of hearing yourself say the words is very powerful and, for many, healing.

How did that make you feel?

....

....

....

....

....

Exercise 5: Naming your baby

As a part of coping with miscarriage, sometimes it helps to give the baby or babies a name as a way of memorialising them. Others choose not to. What feels right for you?

If you do choose to name your baby, here are some things to consider.

Consider a gender-neutral name if the pregnancy loss occurred before it was possible to determine gender. If you had a feeling one way or the other about the baby's gender, you can feel free to give your baby a name suited to that gender. Remember, there are no wrong moves here; you should do what feels right for you and your partner.

Consider using a name that you love but which you would not use for a future baby; or if you had a name already selected for the baby-to-be, you might consider using that name.

Pregnant women often refer to the foetus they're carrying by a nickname. Maybe you referred to your pregnancy as Jellybean or

Peanut? It's okay to keep that name here. Do whatever feels right and best for you.

Consolidation

I hope that you have found some comfort by working through the exercises in this chapter. It's important not to force or rush your journey through the stages of grief – just take it one day at a time. Also know that it's okay to ask for help. Keep in mind that peace and resolution can only be found in letting go. Loss is so very painful, but I want you to keep in mind that things will change and you will change. It won't always hurt the way it does now. I promise you that you will find your way.

I'm going to leave you with one 'at least' that I hope makes a difference:

That in this pain that feels so solitary, at least you're not alone.

Conclusion

Thank you for allowing me to help you on your journey towards the baby in you. I hope that this book has, in some way, helped you to cultivate your own **inner** fertility therapist. You now have the tools and experience you need to nurture your authentic mindset. How does that feel?

Let's take a moment to reflect. What have you learned from this book? What has been important to you? If any of the chapters particularly resonated with you, please revisit them. Just as in a therapeutic setting, we don't just talk about something once and never revisit it. It's an ongoing process. In much the same way, don't think that now you've reached the end of this book you're 'done'. I trust that you will reread the information that's important for you and trust yourself to gravitate toward the right exercises at the right time.

I'd like to conclude by saying how grateful I am that you have invested your time in yourself to work through this book. I feel confident that you now see, as I do, that fertility is not just about your body but is intrinsically connected to your mind.

This book will continue to be there for you, as will I, whenever you need me.

Journal

Date:

How was my sleep?	Poor – OK – Good
How many hours did I sleep for?	6 – 7 – 8 – 9 – 10
What is my energy level like?	Poor – OK – Good
How do I feel my concentration ability is?	Poor – OK – Good
How have I been eating?	Poor – OK – Good
Have I kept myself hydrated?	Poor – OK – Good
How do I feel overall?	Low – OK – Upbeat

Please consider the following statements:

1. What am I feeling?
2. What is my feeling temperature? How do I feel from 1 to 10?
   (10 being anxious, 1 being calm)
3. What am I thinking?
4. What's the proof that it will happen?
5. What's the proof that it won't happen?
6. So what if it happens?
7. How can I deal with it?
8. What can I say and do to help me get through this?
9. What's my feeling temperature now?

Now list three things you're grateful for:

1. ....
2. ....
3. ....

Now list two people you're grateful for:

1. ....
2. ....

Notes:

Notes:

Notes:

....

....

....

....

....

....

....

....

....

....

....

....

....

....

....

....

Notes:

Notes:

....

....

....

....

....

....

....

....

....

....

....

....

....

....

....

....

Notes:

....

....

....

....

....

....

....

....

....

....

....

....

....

....

....

Notes:

....

....

....

....

....

....

....

....

....

....

....

....

....

....

....

....

Notes:

....

....

....

....

....

....

....

....

....

....

....

....

....

....

....

Notes:

....
....
....
....
....
....
....
....
....
....
....
....
....
....
....
....

Notes:

....

....

....

....

....

....

....

....

....

....

....

....

....

....

....

Notes:

....

....

....

....

....

....

....

....

....

....

....

....

....

....

....

....

Notes:

Notes:

....

....

....

....

....

....

....

....

....

....

....

....

....

....

....

....

9 781800 422131